W9-BIF-498

JADE FLUTE

The Story of Chinese Music

JADE FLUTE

The Story of Chinese Music

T.C. Lai · Robert Mok

SCHOCKEN BOOKS · NEW YORK

First American edition published by Schocken Books 1985
10 9 8 7 6 5 4 3 2 1 85 86 87 88

Published by agreement with The Swindon Book Company, Kowloon, Hong Kong

Library of Congress Cataloging in Publication Data
Lai, T.C.
Jade flute.
Bibliography: p.
1. Music – China – History and criticism. I. Mok, Robert. II. Title.
ML336. L118 1985 781.751 84-22923

Printed in Hong Kong
ISBN 0–8052–3961–8

To
Our Fathers

Acknowledgements & thanks
for advice, suggestions and courtesies

Mr. Frederick Fuller
Dr. Fritz Kuttner
Mr. Keith Hunter
Mrs. Pansy Wong
Mr. Ho Tzu
Mrs. Maranda Yeung
Members of Staff of the Library
of the Chinese University of Hong Kong

In this collaboration, Robert Mok did the research on music and wrote the text. T.C. Lai is responsible for the editing and production of the book besides contributing anecdotes, translations of poems and the majority of the illustrations.

春夜洛城聞笛

誰家玉笛暗飛聲散入春風滿洛城此夜曲中聞折柳何人不起故園情

The Jade Flute
Li Po

Whence comes the
faint, fleeting
sound of the
jade flute

Diffusing itself
in the spring
breeze over the
city of Loyang?

On such a night,
hearing the song
*Breaking the
Willow Branch*,

Who can help being
stirred by
thoughts of home?

FOREWORD

The question "What is Chinese music?" has often been asked but the answer is not easy to give. With a history which spans over many thousand years, Chinese music has undergone considerable changes due to racial interaction as a result of wars and conquests. Many books have been written on the subject but they tend to cater to specialists and do not reach the general public. Hence the need for the present volume.

The book is designed as a general description, supported by recent discoveries and research. Anecdotes, poems and numerous illustrations are used so that the book not only gives the reader an idea of what Chinese music is but also how it is related to its culture, literature and art.

Combining the technical with the literary and artistic is not an easy task. The risk is that the result may be too technical for the layman and not learned enough for the specialist. It is hoped, however, that the reader will find here something informative as well as entertaining.

R.M. · T.C.L.

Anecdotes, poems and some short passages that are not organic parts of the main text are set in *italics*. Where desirable, they are separated by woodblock print decorations.

THE CHINESE MUSIC SYSTEM

If you say that music comes from the zither,
Why does it fail to make any sound when kept
in the case?
If you say that music comes from your fingers,
Why don't you listen through the finger tips?

THE CHINESE MUSIC SYSTEM

The Dawn of Chinese Music

Prehistoric China was dominated by god-kings who besides ruling the people, taught the ways of civilization. One of these legendary figures, *Ke T'ien Shih*, a tribal ruler who is supposed to have lived in the third millenium B.C., is said to have created a form of music in which three men waved the tail of an ox, stamped their feet and chanted the *Pa Ch'üeh* – eight songs in praise of the benevolence of the emperor, in giving thanks to Heaven and Earth for good weather and bountiful crops and in worship of certain birds and beasts. It is also said that at the beginning of the reign of *Yin K'ang Shih*, when a great deal of rain swelled the waterways, the people fell into great melancholy and inertia. Hence dancing was created, so that the people could limber up and tone their muscles.

These legends about the earliest musical life in a primitive society were handed down by word of mouth, recorded in bits of oracle bones, but were not described in detail until much later in the writings of Chou and Han dynasties, notably in *Ch'un Ch'iu* (Spring and Autumn Annals) of Lü Pu-wei (ca. B.C. 239). Leaving aside their credibility, they do point to the fact that music and dancing were part of agricultural activities and as suggested by the songs of *Pa Ch'üeh,* they were connected with a totemic culture, in which a non-human object was sometimes asserted to have an ancestral relationship.

Authenticated history did not begin until the *Shang* Dynasty (B.C. 1765?-1121?) when events were reported in oracle bones. These are pieces of animal bones on which early writings were inscribed and a great number of them have been found in excavated sites. Besides oracle bones, certain musical artifacts such as bone whistles and clay flutes were unearthed.(1) These have been studied and their pitch tested in scientific laboratories in China in recent times; certain beliefs about primitive musical life based on legends and pseudo-history can now be either refuted or confirmed by archaeo-musicology.

From oracle bone inscriptions we learn that following periods of heavy rainfall there must have been periods when the climate was exceedingly dry, and praying for rain was a major function of music, the person officiating being a sorcerer who was also a dancer. Many oracle bone inscriptions relate dancing to praying for rain, and the word

Wu 舞 (dance), a homonym of 巫 (sorcery, sorcerer) was written as , suggesting a person dancing with a pair of flapping sleeves. Thus sorcerer-dancers invoke a supernatural power to conquer nature, and to defend themselves and their fellow-men against the harsh elements. Their dancing might even take the form of military exercise to prepare against the intrusion of other nomadic tribes. Dancing in primitive times was a religious rite in the worship of a particular totem, for example, the *Hsuan Niao* – a mythical bird. According to legend, *Chien Ti* swallowed an egg of the *Hsuan Niao* and begot the tribe of the *Shangs*. Another story was told that the Duke of *Sung* (Chou Dynasty) entertained the Marquis of *Ch'in* with the dance-drama *Sang Lin* in which feathered dancers in the guise of the mythical bird presented the epic story of the birth of the *Shang* people. The spectacle must have been weird and frightening, for the Marquis "trembling with fear, beat a hasty retreat to the inner chamber."

In the course of time, it was found that ritualistic music and dancing could be used for private entertainment. Toward the end of the *Hsia* Dynasty (B.C. 2205? – 1762?), it was said – with some exaggeration, perhaps – that the decadent tribal ruler *Chieh* owned 30,000 women entertainers who clamoured at dawn before the Imperial Gate and whose music-making could be heard "in the three thoroughfares of the city." By the time of *Shang*, with the emergence of a slave society, music and dancing had become very much a part of the way of life of the *Shang* rulers, and slaves were trained as professional musicians and dancers. Excavation of *Shang* tombs at *Anyang* and at *Hui Hsien* have yielded musical instruments together with their players, slaves who were buried alive with their departed masters. In spite of the cruelty and excesses of the *Shang* slave society, by that time China's civilization was advancing to a stage where material conditions were conducive to the development of music as an independent art form.

The sound of the fervent chanting of primitive people praying for rain, or of the raucous music-making at the bacchanalia of the *Shang* courts, must now be left to our imagination, with the help of the vivid descriptions found in historical writings. However, archaeological finds corroborated by information from oracle bone inscriptions do provide us with important clues to the musical instruments and the music systems that were in use during these early periods.

The ideographic script on the oracle bone has 壴 or 鼓 for the word *Ku* (drum), symbolizing a drum mounted on a pedestal with or without the player beside it. The *Ch'ing* (sonorous stone chime) was written as [illegible], symbolizing a hung stone chime and its player in the position to strike it with a mallet. A set of primitive raft pipes was represented as [illegible] for the word 籥 (*Yueh*) whose derivative 龢 (*Ho*) has the meaning of 'peace" or "accord", suggesting that the pipes of the *Ho* could have been played simultaneously to create the effect of harmony. There is also the word 樂 (*Yueh* – joy, music) written as [illegible] in oracle bones, which some

Ode to the Shang

How dignified! How splendid!
Let's set up and beat the drums;
Let them roll and let them rumble
To beguile our great ancestors.
Sound the sacrificial music
Ye descendants of T'ang!
May our ancestors give us good health and fortune.
Hear the drums roll and hear them rumble!
Let's play the pipes and obes –
Sweet and soothing –
To the accompaniment of the chime.
Strong descendants of T'ang
Sing your august and mellow songs!
The bells and drums roll and rumble;
Graceful and vigorous are the dances.
Here we have honoured guests and fine –
Rejoicing they are with us all.

from the Book of Songs

scholars believed to symbolize "silk strings attached to a piece of wood", representing a sort of stringed instrument.

Since the oracle bones belong to the second millennium B.C., the actual instruments they allude to could have been in existence much earlier. It is safe to assume that during that time, there was already an array of crude musical instruments capable of producing a series of notes and certain combinations of intervals. It seems that toward the end of the neolithic age, an embryonic concept of melody and scale had dawned upon the Chinese people in primeval times.

By late *Shang,* around the 12th century, B.C., instrument-making had become greatly refined due to the advances of technology. Bells were by this time cast in metal and alloy and lithophone which had been made of rough material was now made of some kind of stone with acoustical properties, artistically shaped and decorated. With these advances, the bells and the stone chimes acquired definite pitch. The crude clay whistles took on a refined oval shape with two to five fingering holes. A number of these instruments have been unearthed at important *Shang* sites, notably at *Anyang* and *Hui Hsien*, Honan Province. There must have been other instruments such as pan pipes, single reed pipes and a variety of drums. Perhaps it is because of the more perishable material of which these were made that none has survived, except in fragments – such as the wooden drum frame unearthed at *Anyang* in 1935.

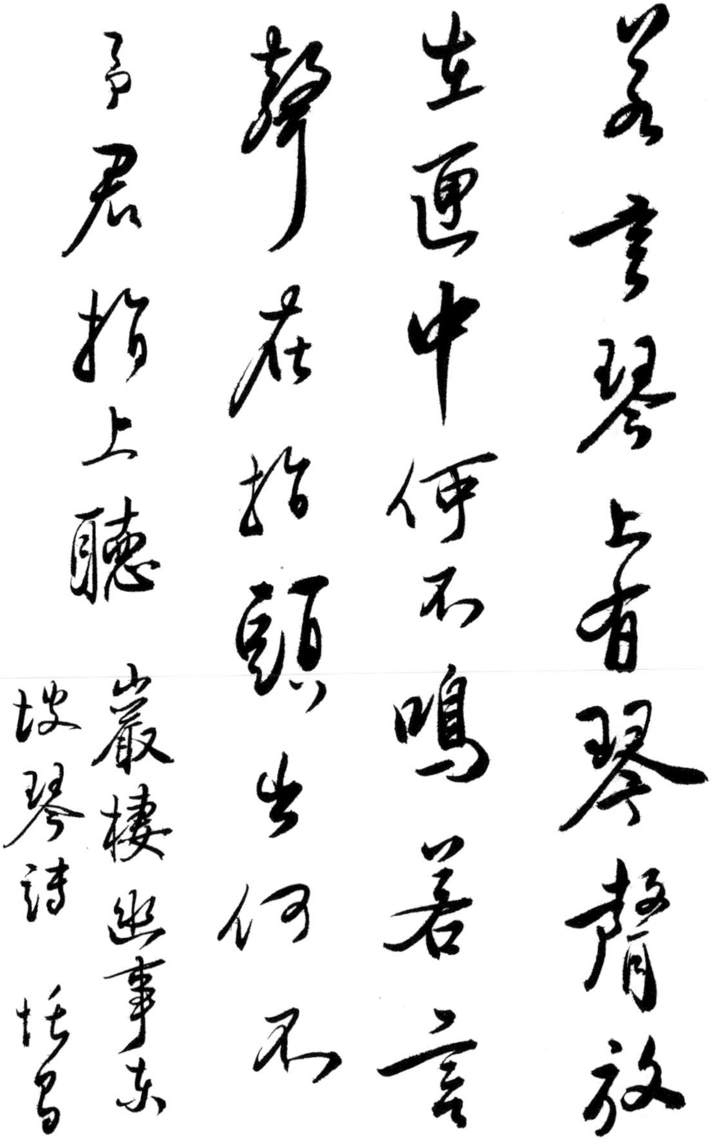

若言琴上有琴聲放
在匣中何不鳴若言
聲在指頭上何不
於君指上聽

巖棲幽事东
坡琴詩

The translation of the poem above is on page 12.

It is interesting to note that bells and sonorous stones of this period were often found in sets of three implying the intervals of major second and major and minor thirds, the foundation of the pentatonic scale, as shown in the following examples(2):

Example 1. A three-unit stone chime in the collection of the Palace Museum in Peking:

Example 2. A set of three bells in the same collection:

Noteworthy among these instruments were the clay *Hsün* (oval clay ocarina) of which three were unearthed from a *Shang* tomb at *Hui Hsien*. Tests made on the two intact smaller ones with five fingering holes respectively show that eleven notes could be produced, using a combination of fingerings. For the purpose of comparison, all the notes the unearthed instruments belonging to this period are capable of producing are listed below, although one may not assume that all of them were used in practice. (2):

Example 3.

a. Single large sonorous stone decorated with tiger stripes
b. Bell chime, Palace Museum
c. Bell chime, Village of *T'a Si K'ung*
d. Stone chime, Palace Museum
e. Small oval clay ocarinas

From the above example, we can see that there are common notes produced by the various instruments. The astonishing consistency in pitch of the two small oval clay ocarinas suggests that the people of *Shang* already had a keen perception of pitch, probably as the result of singing to the accompaniment of musical instruments of definite pitch over a long period of time.

What sort of a music system was it that was used with these instruments and what notes did they produce? One can assume that some kind of scale consisting of three or more notes was in use and perhaps some rudimentary form of transposition as well. One can also imagine the kind of musical scene vividly recounted in the Book of Songs (a collection of folk songs from early Chou Dynasty to the middle period of Ch'un Ch'iu) in an *Ode to Shang* which describes a large force of musicians playing various types of instruments, and singers and dancers in splendid costumes – a far cry indeed from the sorcery dance of the prehistoric age.

Until mathematical calculations for the 12-tone system were devised by Lü Pu-wei in the third century, B.C., there was no evidence that such a system existed or was actually in use in some earlier periods. However, from the pitches produced by excavated instruments from *Shang* tombs and from the fact that names of many pitches in the system were mentioned in connection with early events, one would assume that the people in *Shang* Dynasty already possessed a certain concept of definite pitch. These facts also lend credibility to the legend about how the twelve semi-tones came into being (see p. 23 below) as an example on how practice often comes before theory in human endeavours.

The Chinese Music System

The invention of the Chinese music system was credited to Huang Ti, a legendary figure said to have lived in the third millenium B.C. The story goes that Huang Ti ordered his court entertainer Ling Lun to "create music", whereupon Ling Lun "travelled westwards from the Ta Hsia to the north side of the K'un Lun range and gathered bamboos from the valleys. He selected hollow tubes of uniform bore and cut a length of three *chun** and nine *fen** between the two joints to make a pitch pipe for the tone of *Yellow Bell*. Then he cut twelve other tubes and fix their pitches according to the singing of the *Feng Huang* birds."

This story was first told in *Ch'un Ch'iu* and repeated in other ancient books dealing with music. It matters not whether there was actually such a person as the Yellow Emperor or that this "lo-and-behold" way of inventing a music system has any truth in it. The interesting point in the story is that although the ancient Chinese hit upon the idea of the pitch pipe, they had to rely on the singing of the birds to fix the pitch. This should not be taken as pure fairy tale. Yang Yin-liu the famous Chinese musicologist wrote in his Outline of Chinese Music(3) that he heard the following series of notes from an unknown bird every morning, when he was spending the summer of 1942 in a mountain resort in Szechuan:

* Chinese units of length
Chun: 1/3 decimetre; Fen: 1/3 centimetre

It can be seen that a D Major pentatonic scale is implied in the above series of notes. Other musicians have also reported hearing birds singing scale-like passages in *Huang Shan* and in other places. It may also be recalled that in the 1930s the British cellist Beatrice Harrison used to take her cello into the woods and played to the accompaniment of the nightingales (which sang in unison with her); and she made some recordings which earned her the title of "the Lady of the Nightingale"!

Besides the story of the creation of music, *Ch'un Ch'iu* described the method of producing the twelve tones by what is known as the method of "superior and inferior generation". According to Lü Pu-wei, to generate a "superior" tone, a third is taken off the length of the generator (presumably a pipe), producing a tone a fifth above the fundamental; to generate an "inferior tone", a third of the new length is added to it, producing a tone a fourth below the preceding tone. By the ratios of 3:2 and 3:4, twelve semi-tones are thus "generated". It may be noted, however, that a perfect octave cannot be achieved by this method, the further applications of which will yield a continuous spiral. This method conforms to Pythagoras' principle of calculation":

(a) Superior and inferior generation
(b) Hypothetical gamut of twelve semi-tones

Although this series of ascending fifths and descending fourths making up a gamut of twelve semi-tones appears at first sight to be a chromatic scale, it has not been regarded nor applied as such to Chinese music. However, it is from this "up-and-down" principle that the pentatonic scale and the old heptatonic scale with its raised fourth are theoretically derived.

The scale predominantly used in Chinese music is the five-tone scale. This scale and later the seven-tone scale may have been in practical use through an empirical process long before their theoretical explanations appeared in *Kuan Tzu* (fourth century, B.C.) or *Ch'un Ch'iu*. Ancient Chinese philosophers were prone to explain certain physical phenomena by metaphysical means. In particular, the mystical belief that chronology and numerology had something in common with the music system led them to follow a course by which endless and futile pursuits were made to reconcile the twelve months of the year and other chronological numbers with the twelve tones in the traditional system.

The Chinese tonal system probably would have stopped at the discovery of this method of calculating the twelve semi-tones, if not for the necessity of *Hsuan Kung*, literally "revolving the fundamental tone Kung." This is to say, all the semi-tones may be taken, one after another, as the fundamental, or the Kung, to form a scale. Since Kung, as the first tone in a scale, is to represent the Ruler, its place an octave above must be exactly in the relationship of 2:1 in the frequency of vibration.

This, however, cannot be achieved by further application of the method of Lü Pu-wei. And so the quest for the solution of this problem, that of achieving a perfect octave, led to the proliferation of tonal systems to which the mathematical genius of the ancient Chinese was actively applied. Briefly, these mathematicians attempted a multiple extension of the "up-and-down" principle in the hope of closing the gap of the spiral. Among these musico-mathematicians were Ching Fang in the first century, B.C. who experimented on a string instrument called the Chun, a monochord, and came up with a sixty-tone system; Ch'ien Lo-chih (ca. 438), who went so far as to advocate a 360-tone system to correspond to the number of days in a year; and Ts'ai Yuan-ting in the twelfth century extended the spiral from 12 to 18 steps.

In the meantime, there was the insistent demand for a "new" system of music in every dynasty, in which the fundamental pitch of Kung should differ (however slightly) from the previous one. The confusion that arose in trying to achieve this must have been very great, so much so that a certain Wei Han-chin, in attempting to curry the favour of Emperor Hui Tsung of the Sung Dynasty, silenced all talks about a new music system by simply advocating to base the length of the pipe for the first tone Yellow Bell (Kung) on the measurements of the Emperor's fingers. The quest came to an end by the 16th century when Prince Chu Tsai-yü (ca. 1584) of the Ming Dynasty established the equal temperament of the Chinese scale, eliminating the two sizes of semi-tones in the traditional system. By this time, foreign instruments, notably fretted instruments, were introduced into China and had become popular, so that for practical reasons, equal temperament became a necessity.

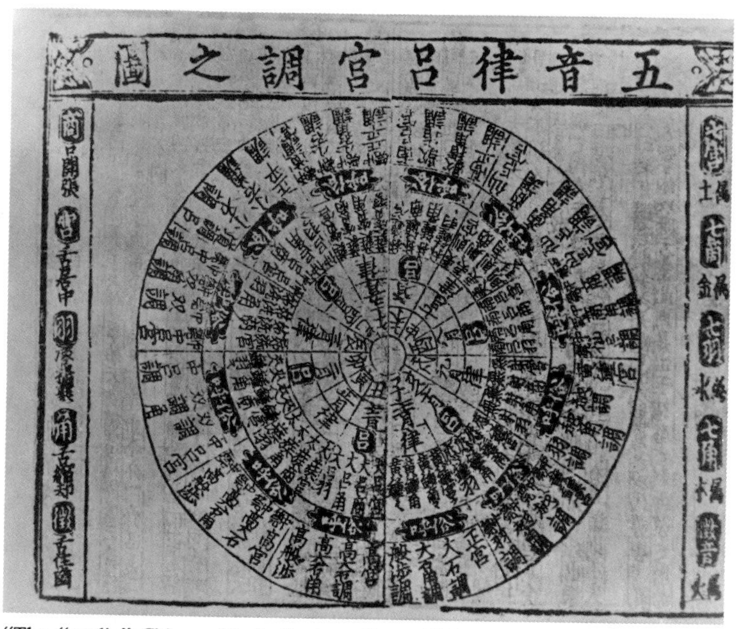

"The "cyclic" Chinese Music System. From *Shih Lin Kuang Chi* by Chen Yuan-liang (ca. 1340).

The ancient Chinese believed that the twelve tones of the *Lü-lü* system went around a cycle like the twelve months of the year, or the twelve hours of the day. This elaborate disk, among many found in treatises on music, lists in each band the twelve tonal units of the *Lü-lü* system with the corresponding months of the years and hours of the day, the five tones of the pentatonic scale (mysteriously, the fifth "*chih*" is not listed), and the names of the scales etc. The idea is that, by revolving the band, each of the twelve tonal units may be used as fundamental of the five-tone scale, yielding 60 five-tone scales (5 × 12) and 84 seven-tone scales (7 × 12) in all. On the sides of the picture are written the names of the intervals of the five-tone scale *Kung, Shan, Chiao, Chih, Yü* and the corresponding five elements metal, wood, water, fire and earth.

Musical Notation.

There is no standard notation for Chinese music. The various methods may be grouped under (1) pitch system (2) descriptive system (3) hand-and-finger system (4) *Kung Ch'e* system (5) rhythmic recitation and (6) numerical system.

The principles on which these system were founded are described briefly as follows:

The oldest of these systems is the *Lü-Lü* system with its six "superior" (ascending fifths) and "inferior" (descending fourths) tonal units, forming a gamut of twelve semi-tones, each with a pitch name. The names of the pitches are:

黃鍾	大呂	太簇	夾鍾	姑洗	仲呂
Huang Chung	Ta Lü	T'ai Ts'u	Chia Chung	Ku Hsi	Chung Lü
蕤賓	林鍾	夷則	南呂	無射	應鍾
Jui Pin	Lin Chung	I Tse	Nan Lü	Wu I	Ying Chung

Several names have the character 鍾 (bell) as the suffix, suggesting that the pitches may have been determined by the bells in a series. Noteworthy also is the fact that such pitch-names as 蕤賓 and 夷則 appear to be of non-*Han* origin, hinting strongly that this oldest Chinese music system may be multi-ethnic in origin.

Since these names relate to the pitches in this

system, the intervals such as those that form a pentatonic scale are named *Kung* (宮), *Shang* (商), *Chiao* (角), *Chih* (徵), *Yü* (羽). For the seven-tone scale, the raised fourth and the seventh are named *Pien Chih* (變徵) and *Pien Kung* (變宮). Any degree of this system may be used as the fundamental – the *Kung* of a given scale. Thus a scale beginning on the pitch of the first degree is the scale of the *Huang-Chung-Kung* and that which begins with the second degree is *T'ai-Ts'u-Kung*, the same way that a Western scale is named after the pitch names of C D E and so forth. The five-tone scale may begin on any of the five tones, yielding five Tiao or modes. Thus a *Yü Tiao* of *Huang-Chung-Kung* is the fifth mode of a five-tone scale whose first degree is in the pitch of the *Huang Chung*. This opens up many possibilities for transposition and choice of modes in Chinese music.

The hand-and-finger system suggests how the player should play his instrument. Special signs (complex) are devised to show the order of strings to strike, the finger holes to cover, positions, fingerings and effects etc. Some signs are written along the pitch-names, and others are placed beside the melodic line indicated, for example, by the *Kung Ch'e* system. In this category, the most complete system is the notation for the *Ch'in* (zither) which will be briefly discussed in the relevant chapter.

The *Kung Ch'e* system is a kind of Chinese solfège system and is based on the seven-tone scale. It may have originated from wind instrument playing, since the Chinese character 合 (to close) for the first note seems to suggest the closing of all the finger holes to produce the tone of a closed pipe.

Other characters such as 六 (six) and 五 (five) also seem to indicate the order of fingering. The following is a scale in the *Kung Ch'e* system:

For the note an octave above the fundamental, the radical 亻(abbreviation for 倍, or double) is added to the character representing the fundamental note, as

The above scale is shown as a diatonic major scale. The scale may be transposed, using a different Chinese character for the tonic.

To mark the time, a simple system of accented and unaccented beats called *Pan-yen* is used. These are usually placed alongside the *Kung-Ch'e* notation. The following is an example(4) of *Chü* singing, showing the use of the *Pan-yen* method(below the *Kung Ch'e* notation):

ㄱ *Pan* Strong Beat
口 *Yen* Weak Beat

Note that the regular beats begin with the second half of the second measure, the two words before the beat begins are to be sung in free meter. Also, the strong beat falls on the word to be stressed, thus given an undulating effect, in the style of *Chü* singing.

In practising music involving percussion, the player recites the rhythmic patterns of the *Lo Ku Ching* (literally, the sutra of the gong and drum), which he has learnt by heart. Compared to the chanting of the sutra by Buddhist monk, *Lo Ku Ching* not only indicates the rhythmic patterns but also simulates the sound of the percussion instruments used, as in the following example:

答 *Ta*: hoop drum – heavy single stroke
台 *T'ai*: small gong
倉 *Ts'ang*: gong, small gong, cymbals together
七 *Ch'i*: small cymbals

Nothing in the traditional system gives precise information on the duration of the beat and the meter of the music. Such inadequacy in the written music does not seem to bother the Chinese musician. It would seem that such sketchy notation like the *Kung Ch'e* system serves as a sort of reminder to the musician as to the general movement of the music. It is of little importance whether a note receives a beat more or less or whether the notes are tied or not. A tune has many variants according to the particular school of playing and is usually memorized by the player.

Modern teaching in school calls for more accurate notation, especially in group singing and playing. At the turn of the century, a system based essentially on the principles of the tonic-so-fa and the numerical notation of the Frenchman Emile Chevé was introduced from Japan and has been in popular use ever since. In this system, *do* is represented by 1 as the tonic of a given key, and the sequence of *re, mi, fa, so, la, si* by the numerals 2, 3, 4, 5 and 7. An octave above is indicated by a dot above the numeral and an octave below by a dot below the numeral. Naturally, this system is more suited for monophonic music.

TRADITIONS OF CHINESE MUSIC

TRADITIONS OF CHINESE MUSIC

For a music to have survived more than three thousand years of recorded history, there must be a strong basis for its existence. The tumultuous history of ancient China with its many twists and turns and great upheavals was certainly not conducive to the uninterrupted development of music. There is besides a conspicuous lack of such catalytic factors as the Christian Church or *Ars Nova* which help to shape the development of Western music. In primitive times, Chinese music shares the same characteristics of the musics of other primitive cultures. Music is mostly a means to counteract supernatural forces – to calm the wrath of nature, to appease the gods and to appeal to them for such acts of benevolence as the vouchsafing of rainfall, good weather, immunity from plagues and so forth, through its performance.

However, civilization soon did away with these crude superstitions and as music became a part of human activities, it was subjected to socio-political influence and was often put to use for a definite purpose. Against this was the natural tendency to express human feelings through music and the purely sensuous enjoyment of it. The character of Chinese music and its development were affected by certain factors which are discussed below.

The Philosophical Basis of Chinese Music

The early formation of different schools of thought affected the course of Chinese music in that they tended to define its nature and its functions according to their precepts. Briefly, these main schools of thought which influenced music are grouped under their founders: (1) Lao Tzu (2) Mo Tzu and (3) Confucius. These philosophers took the view that man's desire for music is as strong as his lust for woman and his love for good food. Excessive indulgence in it for personal pleasure, they believed, brought down many a powerful ruler in the past. Desire for music therefore must be regulated and constrained. These rulers, it was alleged, neglected the affairs of state, indulging in the delights of women and music. And so Lao Tzu decided against it. Moreover, he preached "Wu Wei" (non-assertion) and prevailed upon the people to "return to a state of nature". Such a human endeavour as music-making, particularly the systematization of music-making, was considered artificial and contrary to his precept. Lao Tzu said: "Colours blind the eyes, tones deafen the ears and flavours numb the palate". Ironically, in later days, a superstitious cult usurping the name of Taoism used music as a means of self-propagation. "Taoist music" as it is known today has nothing to do with Taoism as conceived by Lao Tzu

Mo Tzu advocated "universal love", "mutual benefit" and "equal distribution of wealth". Music was considered "unproductive" and therefore "unnecessary" and "wasteful". He said: "music is a source of evils and a hindrance to human progress. Therefore, it must be suppressed."

While Lao Tzu and Mo Tzu were essentially anti-music in their thinking, Confucius was not. He held a moralistic view on music. He realizedthat music as a potent force could be made to serve useful ends. As a counsellor to various rulers vying for hegemony during the Warring States period (B.C. 481-256), he wanted music to serve their purpose, that of "regulating" the people and the affairs of the state and, in a larger context, of achieving universal harmony. He therefore saw in music metaphysical as well as socio-political significance. He frowned upon music that gives expression to human desires and feelings. He called this music "*Cheng Sheng*" (wanton music), fearing that it may lead to corruption and excesses. This view about music is perhaps most cogently expressed in the following quotation from Hsün Tzu, a strong adherent of the Confucian school of thought: "the dazzle of a beautiful woman and the music of *Cheng* induce wanton thoughts; on the other hand, watching formally the dance of *Shao* and listening to eulogic music of *Wu* put people in a proper frame of mind. Therefore, the righteous

◀ **The Master on the Apricot Rostrum.** Woodblock print.

Hsin T'an (literally apricot rostrum) was the spot where Confucius taught his disciples who are seen in this woodcut chanting to the playing of the *Ch'in* (seven-string zither) by the master. Some of the songs in the collection *Shih Ching* (Book of Songs) were believed to be zither tunes.

In the Sung Dynasty, there was a strong movement to revive ancient music. "*Shih Yueh*" (Confucian songs set to tunes) was made up after ancient models. The music is modal and is characterized by a very slow tempo, one word to a note. The following is an example of *Shih Yueh*, a reconstruction of a zither tune in the time of Confucius.

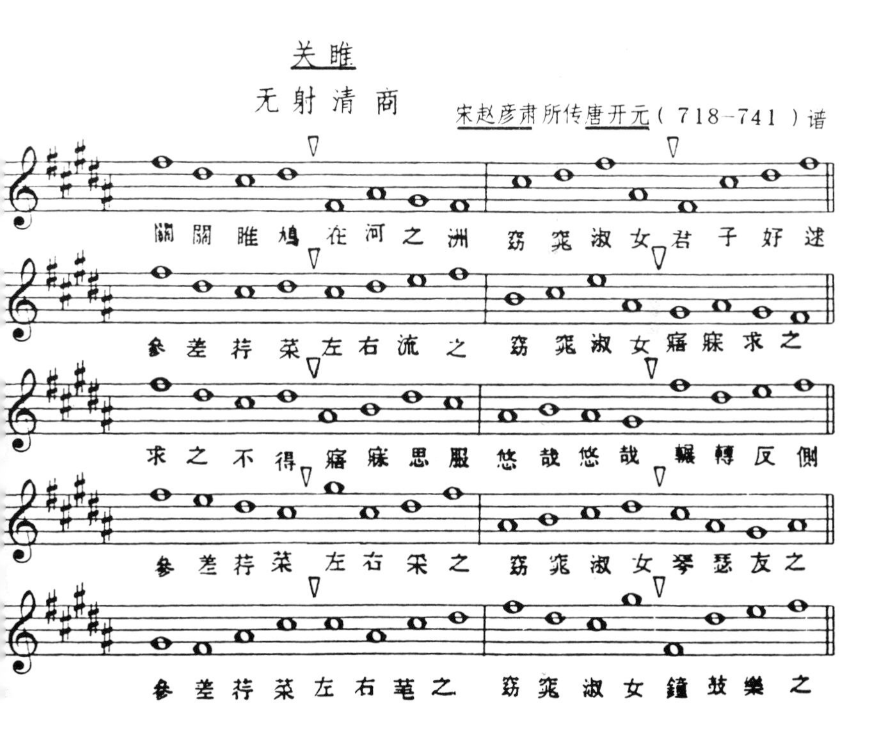

man should not listen to wanton music and turn his eyes from feminine beauty."

Music that Confucius preferred and actively promoted was to be "virtuous", the kind that was performed in worship of the deity or sung in praise of benevolent rulers. Music making then, was not for entertainment but for ritualistic purposes. Moreover, he laid down the qualifications for music-making, for he said in his "Book of the Golden Mean" that "those who do not have the virtue commensurating with his position are not fit to make music, neither are those who have the position but not the virtue."

These concepts led to the creation of a body of music called *Ya Yueh.*

Ya Yueh was founded on mystical and cosmological concepts, such as the concepts of *Yin* and *Yang*, of transcendantal values and numerical significance etc. Chinese recorded history is charged with writings on music based on these concepts. Yet it must not be assumed that all these writings were done by star-gazers. These mystical concepts had given rise to some very interesting and original accoustico-mathematical experiments on a multitude of tonal systems, as mentioned in the previous chapter, which later became subjects of absorbing interest to many modern scholars.

The Pure and the Vulgar

These notions are represented by the Chinese words *Ya* and *Su*. *Ya* is virtually untranslatable, meaning pure, elegant and what is in good taste; and *Su* means common and vulgar. *Ya Yueh*, the pure music, is often taken for music of a classical tradition, although by strict definition, it is the ritual music of the court and the temple. On the other hand, most other types of music, especially folk music, come under the denomination of *Su Yueh*.

In ancient times, what was *Ya* or *Su* in music was not clearly defined. The famous *Yueh Fu* (Bureau of Music) established by Emperor Wu Ti of the Han Dynasty (ca. B.C. 140) was charged with collecting folk songs and to set them to music. These songs have always been regarded as classics. The songs compiled by Confucius in *Shih Ching* were considered quite *Ya* although, ironically, a good many of them are about wooing and mating, scornfully dismissed otherwise as the kind heard "behind the mulberry bushes". The distinction between *Ya* and *Su* music was brought about by the rigid social stratification in a feudal system which Confucius himself had championed. With the emergence of the gentry class – the "mandarins" – music became one of the Six Arts (*Liu Yi*) (5) to be cultivated as befitting their social station, and gentlemen of proper rearing were not supposed to touch the music of the entertainers, which was deemed unfit for the "hall of dignity".

Music that serves ceremonial purposes was properly called *Ya Yueh* , and it was the formal or official music of the court. The guardian of this music was usually a high official of the court who was less concerned with its musical contents than with its ritualistic aspects. And since an important function of *Ya Yueh* was to sing the praise not only of the present but also of past dynasties, whose rulers were of the Han race, it had to be kept free of "impurities" and above all from alien influences. In this way, *Ya Yueh* was isolated from other musical trends and had failed to develop.

Formal ritual music must have become so dull compared with the music of the common people that the Duke of Wei (ca. B.C. 350) once complained to his adviser Tzu Hsia: "I adjust my diadem and listen respectfully to ancient ritual music, but cannot help falling asleep. Why is it that I am never tired of listening to the music of Cheng and Wei?"(6) *Ya Yueh* seems to have degenerated further by the T'ang Dynasty so much so that it was observed in *Li Yueh Chi* (Book on Rites and Music) that "the *T'ai Ch'ang* (music official) relegates those musicians unfit to teach other kinds of music to learn *Ya Yueh.*"

The great bulk of music that came down to us to day is folk music, music that reflects the ways of life of the people and is deeply rooted in entertainment. Like all music of this type, it might have begun quite innocently from imitation of the sounds of nature to the music of wandering village story-tellers. With the establishment of urban centers, it developed into music of the theatre. Competition led to the development of instrumental techniques. The display of virtuosity that we often witness today in the performance of Chinese instruments is the result of many years of cultivation by generations of professional entertainers. The richest tradition of *Su Yueh* is vernacular music of which hundred of types exist today, from musical story-telling, simple and elaborate, to fully-staged music drama, all with distinctive local flavours both as regards speech and musical styles.

Another important notion is that of *Ku* (the ancient past). Nostalgia for what was good in the past – the good old days – is perhaps universal, but for the Chinese, the term *Ku* implies something time-honoured, some heirloom of the glorious past. It was when the country was weakened by internal strife and alien intrusion that the people's imagination turned to periods in the past when China was strong, unified and prosperous. Invariably a "*Fu Ku*" movement (to revive the past) emerged. The rise of neo-Confucianism was just such a movement in the Sung Dynasty and it brought about a type of *Pseudo-Ya Yueh* called *Shih Yueh*, claiming origin in Confucius' times. "*Ku*" then became analogous with "classical" and Chinese classical music, meaning music of the gentry, claims to have its basis in the music of ancient times. While such notions are often taken for defining musical styles, they rarely apply to the contents of the music itself. Music of a popular origin would become classical when it was patronized by the gentry and so, many popular tunes became "ancient classical tunes." On the other hand, since so much ancient music has not been committed to paper, a lot of ancient tunes must indeed have found their way to popular music performances through the ages and have survived to this day under various disguises.

Confucius was playing the Sê, a twenty-five-string zither, when Tzu Kung, a disciple, approached him in a rather grievous and awkward mood. Confucius waited for Tzu Kung to speak. The latter began: "Tsang and I were listening to your playing and he was commenting upon what the music conveyed to him. He sensed in your music some strains of wolfish avarice and malice. I quite agree with him."

Confucius sighed and said, "How admirable! Tsang is indeed a rare sage and has fine ears. Just now when I was playing the Sê, I saw a rat being hunted by a wild cat. The rat went up a house-beam, out of reach of the wild cat, which nevertheless poised itself to prepare for the attack. At that moment, I tried to capture in sound the mood of the wild cat. No wonder Tsang sensed something that reminded him of the avaricious wolf. It was said in the Book of Odes*: 'The bell and the drum within the palace will be heard without.'*

Confucius was standing in the hall one morning when he heard someone weeping very bitterly. Confucius tried to recreate the mood on the zither. When he came out, he heard one of his disciples making a sound of disapproval. Upon inquiring who did it, Yen Hui said, "It was me."

"Why did you do it?" asked Confucius.

Yen answered: "Here was someone who wept bitterly. His sorrow was caused not only by the death of someone but also the imminent departure of someone else."

"How do you know that?" asked Confucius.

"Because its sadness was like that of the bird of Wan Shan which has four fullfledged off-spring. When they were leaving for the wide world, the parent bird saw them off in great sorrow, knowing that once gone they would never return."

Confucius sent someone to inquire of the cause of the weeping, and the reply was: "My father died and I have no money to give him a burial. So I have arranged to sell my son who is even now leaving me."

The Multi-ethnic Tradition

When one speaks of Chinese culture, be it arts or letters, one is not always aware that it is the culture of the Han, as distinct from other racial groups, that is being referred to. From very ancient times, the Hans had held the center of civilization, as settlers of a stable agricultural society in the northern plains and in the fertile Yangtze valleys. A high state of civilization however does not always imply military might. It turns out then during many periods of Chinese history, the refined living and high material standard of the Hans had tempted the intrusion of the plundering barbarians, nomadic peoples of other ethnic origins, who after coming into contact with the Hans shed their ways and became "civilized" themselves. The fact that all these nomadic races became Han-oriented to the extent of giving up their own tongues and adopting Han names explains why they made little impression on the culture of the Hans.

In music however, it is a rather different story. While battles were fought and peace made, the common people both of Han and other races had already freely mingled with one another in their daily undertakings and came to know each other's musical expressions. The lively and uninhibited and therefore more openly expressive music of the nomads were greatly appreciated by the common folks of the Han race whose own music, in contrast, must have been of a more sedate nature. *Hu Yueh*, the 'music of the barbarians,' soon became a distinctive type. Emissaries, often in the person of some royal courtesan dispatched to appease the barbarians, also brought back – if they returned at all – the music of other races which exerted strong influence on the music of the Han people.

Hu Yueh though officially frowned upon as having an adulterating influence on the music of the Hans, nevertheless gained great popularity. By the time of the Han Dynasty, when military power was at its height, the Hans reached out in all directions, conquering large stretches of land beyond their traditional borders, thereby coming into contact with the peoples of Central Asia and other regions.

The mass influx of foreign musical cultures, however, did not come about until after the fifth century, culminating in the T'ang Dynasty, a period of prosperity for 300 years. Buddhism was then only recently introduced into China via the trade routes south of the great Tienshan range. Islamic culture was brought by envoys of lesser nations via the northern routes. At the height of this period of musical interaction, aptly called by historians the Great International Period, ten "departments" of music were officially proclaimed. These comprised the traditional music of the Hans, the music of the nomadic tribes and the music of India, Persia and of many regions in the general area known as Turkestan, resulting in a proliferation of music systems and musical instruments. Kings and princes were known to succumb to the epicurian appeal of the music and dance from these foreign lands (and as a result to lose their thrones). The common people were moved by their great vitality and expressiveness. Yet their music was not to be transplanted unmodified on Chinese soil. It was slowly but steadily absorbed and assimilated in the music of the Hans. Today, after more than a thousand years, Chinese music still bear the stamp of these "foreign" musics, notably in the use of certain modes, in musical instruments and in the formation of the orchestra.

An important fact to be borne in mind is that China has long been a multi-racial nation. Ethnic races such as Tibetans, the Uighurs and the Kazaks in Sinkiang who once were foreigners have become Chinese citizens living in their own country. Nomadic peoples as well as those of other enthnic origins are no longer "barbarians" but are equals of their Han brethren. The multi-ethnic character of Chinese music is the result of a historical process which seems to be repeating itself as Chinese music comes into contact with European music. A new era in the history of Chinese music will be ushered in when the best of the East and the West will be successfully blended into something fresh and beautiful.

Playing Music Together. Ch'iu Ying, 1500–1550 A.D.

The painting depicts an ensemble of musicians in Sung Dynasty (10th to 13th centuries). Sitting on a mat, the musicians dressed in Chinese costumes played musical instruments of mixed origins. The scene reminds one of the *Tso Pu Chi* (literally, sit-down ensemble), a form of "chamber music" with strong alien influence.

Music, Dancing and Acrobatics in Ancient China. Line-drawing of a rubbing from a bas-relief of West Han Dynasty (3rd Century B.C.)

This bas-relief entitled "A Hundred Kinds of Game", unearthed in 1954 in Shantung, unfolds a dramatic panorama featuring jugglers, dancers and musicians in great details. In this section, three rows of musicians are shown sitting on mats. In the first row, four women singers accompanying themselves on the *Wa P'ing* (earthern

hand drum), while a fifth (also appears also to be a woman) seems to be beating time with something in her hand. In the second row are players of *Hsün* (globular clay flute), *Pai Hsiao* (pan pipes) and *Nao* (single large bell). In the third row, one musician plays the *Yü* (mouth organ), another the *Se* (zither), while the one with his hand covering the mouth appears to be playing a kind of Jew's harp (possibly with a leaf as the reed – "*Chui Yeh*"). The one without instrument is probably a singer. At the back of the orchestra, two large bells on a rack are seen being rammed by a player with a rod hung from a frame. Behind him, another player, also on a mat, is seen playing a stone chime with a striker. A *Chien Ku* (barrow drum) mounted on an elaborate stand with mystic birds and tassles is being struck by a player with flapping arms. Two jugglers, one balancing a cross from which dangle little figures (thought to be little children doing somersaults); another is seen juggling with daggers and balls. The dancer with a pair of flying sleeves is looking backwards towards seven drums (*Pan Ku*) on the ground on which he will presently mount and stamp rhythmically to the music. Although bell and stone chimes as well as the large zither (*Sê*) later became instruments for playing ritual music for the court and the temple, they were once used for popular entertainment as shown in this bas-relief. Two instruments, the *Yü* and the *Sê* were unearthed in mint condition from a Han tomb at Ma Wang Tui in 1973.

The remarkable graphic presentation of this bas-relief provides much valuable information about music and dancing in ancient China.

The common belief that zither music is necessarily ya, *is a mistake. On the contrary, zither music used to be that of* Cheng *and* Wei. *Today what is called* Cheng *and* Wei *is foreign music, not Chinese. Since the reign of T'ien Pao, the central sitting and standing sections of an orchestra are indistinguishable from the foreign instrumental section. Some say that the pi-pa is Chinese Cheng-wei (folk) music but none can say with certainty.*

(Su Shih)

PA YIN – THE EIGHT KINDS OF SOUND

PA YIN – THE EIGHT KINDS OF SOUND

A lady who heard Chinese music for the first time was once asked about her impression of it. "Oh, that bamboo and butterfly music", she said, "I just love its colourful sounds!" For all her musical naivety, her comment was quite apt. "Bamboo and Butterfly music" suggests a kind of music that has a strong affinity with nature, and that goes for Chinese instrumental music. With European music, it has always been said that musical instruments tend to imitate the human voice. The violin or the oboe playing a *cantilena* passage is said to imitate singing, and listening to such a passage played on them, one does not usually think of the properties of the materials these instruments are made of. Rather, it is the singing quality produced by them that is uppermost in the mind of the listener.

The sounds of Chinese musical instruments suggest something rather different. The sounds of the *Ti*, the bamboo cross flute with a thin membrane as the vibrating element, the *Ch'in*, the zither with seven silk strings, and the sonorous stone and bell chimes, have qualities that distinctively relate to the materials they are made of. The sounds of bamboo, silk, stone or bronze defy exact definition, but few would disagree that their sounds are more "elemental" and that they are closer to nature than the human voice.

The ancient Chinese catagorized their instruments according to the materials they are made of. The term *Pa Yin,* the eight kinds of sound, refers to the following eight kinds of materials: *Chin* (metal), *Shih* (stone), *T'u* (earth), *Ke* (hide), *Szu* (silk), *Mu* (wood), *Pao* (gourd) and *Chu* (bamboo). Such a classification leaves much to be desired, since musical instruments are often made of more than one kind of material. For practical reasons, we would abide by the Sachs-Hornbostel classification of chordophone, aerophone, membranophone and idiophone.

An exhaustive listing of the instruments is not possible both because there are many variants to one instrument, and their names often changed from dynasty to dynasty. However, an attempt may be made to list the chief members of each category by their generic names, including some instruments which are now obsolete but historically important. Instruments of the ethnic minorities of China to which many of those listed are related, are not included in this listing.

CHORDOPHONE

Zither:	*Ch'in, Cheng, Sê, K'ung Hou* (obsolete) Materials – bamboo, wood, silk (string)
Fiddle:	*Hu Ch'in* – two-string vertical fiddle in various sizes. Also *Szu Hu* with four strings and *Chui Hu* with a long fingerboard. Materials – bamboo, wood, coconut shell, skin (snake and python for the surface of the sound box), horse hair (bow), silk (string)
Lute:	*P'i-P'a* and its variants Materials – wood, silk (string).
Drum Guitar:	*San Hsien* and its variants. Materials – wood, skin (snake), silk (string)
Round Guitar:	*Yüan* in various sizes, *Yueh Ch'in*, *Shuang Ch'ing.* Materials – wood, silk (string), bone (plectrum).
Dulcimer:	*Yang Ch'in* Materials – wood, metal (string), bamboo (strikers)

AEROPHONE

Globular flute:	*Hsün* (obsolete) ocarina Materials – clay, bone
Vertical flute:	*Hsiao* and its variants

Cross flute: *Ti* and its variants
Material – bamboo

Pandean pipes: *Pai Hsiao* (obsolete)
Material – bamboo

Mouth Organ: *Shêng* and its variants
Materials – bamboo, gourd, metal (for the bowl in modern version and for the free reeds)

Short Oboe: *Kuan, Sona*
Materials – bamboo, reed, brass (for the bell of the Sona)

Trumpet: Long and curved trumpets, *La Pa, Hao Tung* (obsolete)

MEMBRANOPHONE

Drums of various sizes and shapes with surface made of hide and snake skin.

IDIOPHONE

Bell: *Chung* and its variants. Single or as a chime.
Material – metal

Sonorous stone: *Ch'ing,* Single or as a chime.
Material – jade stone

Glockenspiel: *Fang Hsiang* – metal chime mounted on a frame.
Yün Lo – brass cymbal-chime mounted on a frame.

Clappers, woodblocks, gongs and cymbals

In the Chordophone group, metal strings are now commonly used instead of silk strings for larger volume of sound. Modern instruments are made according to accoustical principles, resulting in great improvement of quality.

Diversion of the Gentry. Detail of a *Ming Dynasty Painting 14th-17th century*

Two gentlemen are seen engaged in a little after-dinner diversion, one playing the vertical flute and the other listening appreciatively. Accompanying the master are two young servants, one with a pair of clappers, the other playing the *Hu Ch'in*, the 'barbarian fiddle'. The *Hu Ch'in*, as its name implies, is a non-indigenous instrument, but it is not known when exactly it was introduced into China. This is one of the early paintings in which the *Hu Ch'in* made its appearance.

A chime of bronze bells (Pien Chung) with the inscription 'Keng Hsi', 770-476 B.C. (unearthed in Hunan in 1957)

The Chinese are conscious of the timbre of their instruments. In old treatises on music, when an instrument is referred to in a piece of music, it is sometimes not called by its proper name alone. For example, a *Ti* is called Ti-Sê, or "flute-colour" and *Kuan*, a short oboe, is "*Kuan-Sê*" or "oboe-colour". Colour then, and not merely the sound of an instrument, is considered important. When an instrument is capable of producing a firm and clear sound, it is also said that the instrument has the sound of "*Chin Shih*", the sound of gold and jade stone. *Pa Yin*, the eight kinds of sound produced by the instruments playing together, as in an orchestra, preserve their own identities and distinctive timbres, forming a gossamer of sounds more varied than the homogeneous string or brass choirs of the Western orchestra.

The origin of Chinese musical instruments is heterogeneous. The zithers, bells and sonorous stones, drums, globular flutes, raft pipes and mouth organs date back to time immemorial. They are sometimes referred to as indigenous instruments, meaning those that belong to the Han race, the majority Chinese race who settled in ancient times in the northern plains of China. They are attributed in historical sources to the "invention" of some legendary figures in prehistoric China, and ideograms of these instruments are found on oracle bones of 16th century B.C. In a recent excavation of a tomb of the Western Han Dynasty more than 2000 years ago, a mouth organ (*Yü*), a set of pitch pipes and a zither (*Zê*) were unearthed, the latter with all its strings and bridges intact. Others are attributed to the nomads who were ethnically non-

Han. These include many reed instruments like the Ti, the cross flute, *Hu Chia*, a bamboo bugle, *Pi-li* and *Kuan*, bamboo oboes and a horizontal harp by the name of *K'ung Hou*. From the fifth century onwards, a variety of instruments was brought into China through the great trade routes by foreign envoys who came to pay homage to the Chinese court. These include such instruments as the ovoid *P'i-p'a*, the vertical angular harp and many types of wind and percussion instruments from Central and Southern Asia. Historically, these instruments of non-Han origin are lumped together and called "Hu (literally, barbarian) instruments", while others are called "Islamic instruments". Their Chinese names sometimes betray their origin. For example, *Surnay*, a double-reed Turkish oboe became *Sona*, and *Cank*, the ancient Persian harp, became *K'ung Hou* or *Can Hou*. Pan pipes, the *Lai*, prototype of the *Pai Hsiao* existed in as early as the Shang Dynasty, 15th century B.C. Pan pipes that are played today in the Balkans are called *Niau*. Many of these instruments – at least in their crude form – were commonly found in primitive cultures in all parts of the world. Such inter-migratory movements of musical instruments should present the modern anthropologist with interesting case studies.

When one thinks of how these musical instruments were brought into China from other lands, one is tempted to classify them as non-indigenous instruments, whereas it is more precise to call them instruments of non-Han origin, considering the fact that China has always been a multi-racial nation. In any case, all of them have become "sinicized" for more than a thousand years, so that the Chinese

Stone Chime. Temple of Heaven, Peking

Sixteen L-shape sonorous stones mounted on an elaborate stand are arranged in two rows according to the *Lu-lü* system. Twelve sonorous stones are a half-tone apart, and the addition six units are an octave below the ninth, tenth, eleventh and twelveth units in the series. Made during the reign of Chien Lung, (18th Century), they are of uniform size, graduating in thickness to determine the pitch of each unit.

Bell Chime. Temple of Heaven, Peking

Sixteen bells of uniform size, graduating in thickness, are mounted in the same way as the stone chime. Made in the same period, both the bell and the stone chimes were used in ritual music.

can rightfully claim them as their own. Yet the Chinese orchestra today, with a prominent section of plucked instruments, still bears certain resemblance to the orchestra of Middle Eastern countries, reminding us of the cultural interaction with Central Asia that took place many centuries ago.

Musical instruments became obsolete through disuse. Stone and bell chimes and the large zither (Sê) were at one time popular instruments used in a large orchestra to accompany dancing and acrobatics. Since they became exclusive ritual instruments playing the kind of music which had failed to develop, they are rarely heard today, except on such rare occasions as in the annual Confucian rites, when they were dusted and taken out from storage for a public performance by amateurs. So are *La Pa* and *Hao T'ung,* once prominent in military and ceremonial processions, but are now relegated to the museum.

Many instruments of earlier periods did not survive. The *K'ung Hou,* a Persian angular harp somehow failed to gain permanent acceptance in China, although it was once a popular instrument and held its place in the orchestra. The *Fang Hsiang,* a metal chime mounted on a frame was superceded by the *Yün Lo*, a cymbal-chime. The *Ya Cheng,* a bowed zither had passed on to Korea. Instruments that survive to the present time are those which have enjoyed popularity among the people, playing *Su Yueh,* particularly those which found themselves in the practised hand of the professional entertainer. In this regard, the *Chiao Fang* (Teaching

A bell from a chime of sixteen in the Temple of Heaven, with the pitch-name "*Pei Wu Yi*" (lower octave of Wu Yi) engraved on it.

A Sonorous Stone. (11th Century B.C.)

Unearthed in 1950 from an ancient tomb of Yin Dynasty in Anyang, Honan Province, it was made of jade stone, beautifully decorated with "tiger stripes". The earliest musical instrument in existence, it still emits a clear tone of fine quality when struck with a mallet.

Pien-ch'ing. From *Lü Lü Ch'üan Shu* (1596) by Chu Ts'ai-yu.

Court) and the *Li Yüan* (Pear Garden), both schools for entertainers, did much to popularize the instruments and to the development of their playing technique. Many ancient instruments came down in their original form. The *Ch'in*, the *Ti* and the *Hsiao*, for examples, have remained practically unchanged through the ages, while others like the *P'i-P'a* or the *Hu Ch'in* underwent rather drastic changes in construction in the hands of the Chinese. The latter especially, whose prototype may have been the *Kamancheh* of Persia is uniquely Chinese in that the bow passes between its two strings and has a piece of snake skin as the vibrating surface of the sound box.

Chinese literature is rich in allusions to music and musical instruments. The tone colour of certain instruments like the *Ti* or the *Ch'in* seems to be able to excite the imagination of the poet. The jade flute, fittingly played by a lady, evokes a bitter-sweet feeling, while the sound of the metal flute was credited with being able to "pierce the clouds and rend hard granite", and was often associated with the disgruntled or someone who has fallen out of favour of the court, roaming the market place disguised as a beggar.

Anecdotes connected with music abound in literature. One concerns Lung Yü, the beautiful daughter of the duke of Ch'in. Lung Yü was a talented flute player. On one occasion as soon as she put her lips to the flute, the sound generated a whiff of cool breeze. As she continued playing, a rainbow rose over the horizon. Then, a pair of fairy phoenixes arrived to listen. When Lung Yü married Hsiao

Lung Yü playing the Pai Hsiao. Woodblock Print

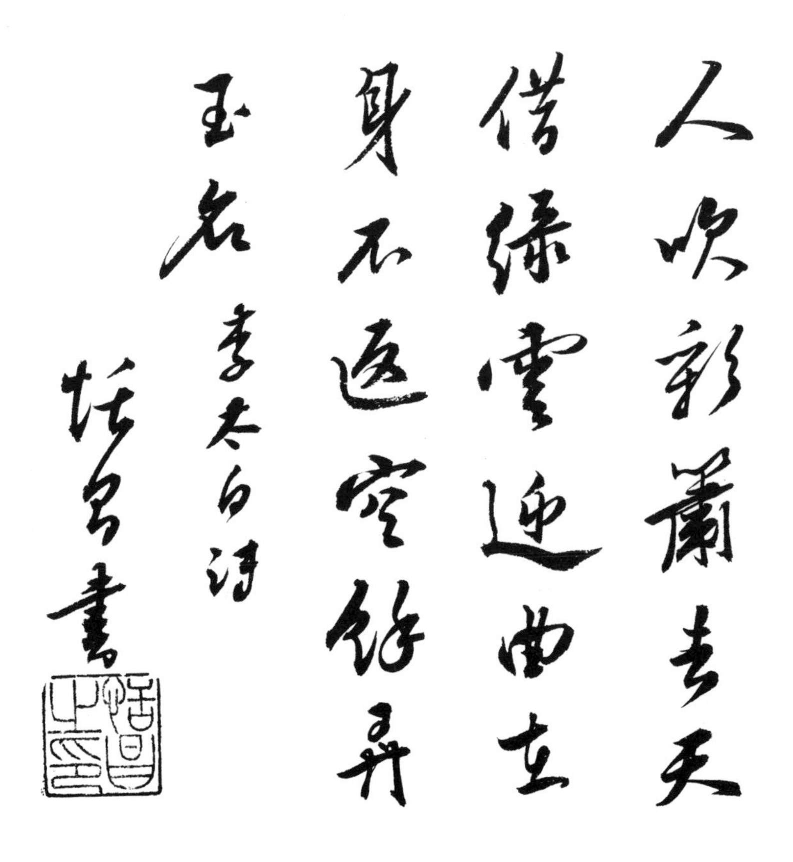

Phoenix Terrace Song

Li Po

Gone they are – he with his many-hued flute
To the heavens with welcoming green clouds.
The tunes still linger here, but she is absent
Leaving behind only the name of Lung Yü.

Playing the flute. Woodblock print.

Shih, also a fine flute player, the duke built for them a pavilion, called the Phoenix Pavilion. One day, they were seen ascending to heaven with a Phoenix and their beautiful music has been heard echoing in the sky ever since. This story so inspired Li Po that he wrote the poem "The Phoenix Terrace Song".

Music and poetry sometimes ally themselves to depict changing times more powerfully than the historian's pen. When the northern plains of China were subjected to frequent intrusions of the nomads, the plaintive sound of certain reed instruments evoked in the mind of the poet the bleak expanse beyond the rampart which stood in lonely guard against the marauding tribes. The sadness of the banished, the hardship of life at the outposts, homesickness and despair are conveyed in many a famous line of the T'ang poets. In contrast, there were other instruments which are associated with a more stable and civilized environment. The zither and the mouth-organ (*Sheng*), traditionally of the Han people, were played by ladies in elegant chambers or in the intimacy of the boudoir. Yet even in this tranquil setting, the music was not devoid of melancholy, for the player was often one whose husband was dispatched to the frontiers to fight the barbarians!

By the time of the T'ang Dynasty, China had emerged as a united and powerful nation having overthrown the Hus who for some time had control of the country.

The Hus became naturalized and adopted the customs of the Hans, influenced as they were by the civilization of a stable feudal society. On the other hand, the Hans found some of the ways of the Hus agreeable and a period of heavy intermingling of the races followed. Against a background of peace and prosperity, the intriguing rhythms and vitality of the alien music and dance, championed often by a pleasure-loving Emperor and his court, had thrived among the Chinese. Who was to sing the praise of the new music but the great epicurian Li Po, himself a half-breed! In his many bacchanalian songs, he divulged a wealth of information on the musical instruments and the kind of music which had left indelible expressions that have formed part of the music of China.

If musical instruments tell anything historically significant, none are more important than the *Ch'in* (the seven-string zither) and the *P'i-P'a,* (the ovoid lute), being instruments with the most developed playing technique, each endowed with a rich repertoire handed down in printed form. The *Ch'in,* an instrument that has survived more than 2500 years, is symbolic of the growth of traditional music, and the *P'i-P'a* is a carrier of alien musical culture, whose influence had gone far beyond the confines of the Middle Kingdom.

Women Entertainers. From "*An Evening of Entertain*ment *with Han Hsi-tsai*" by Ku Hung-chung.

The man beating time with a pair of clappers is believed to be Li Chia-ming, the Deputy Court Music Director.

"Pear Garden" – Women Musicians. Part of a large scroll attributed to Chou Wen-chu (circa 900)

The "Pear Garden" was established by the Emperor Hsuan Tsung of T'ang Dynasty as a school to train entertainers who would perform for his private pleasure. Chou Wen-chu who lived some two hundred years later apparently tried to reconstruct a scene of the "Pear Garden" with an all-women orchestra. Typically, the instruments identified in the painting, metallophone (glockenspiel), harp, cross flute, short oboe, vertical flute, mouth organ, zither, clappers and a variety of percussion instruments are of mixed, Chinese and foreign, origins.

也

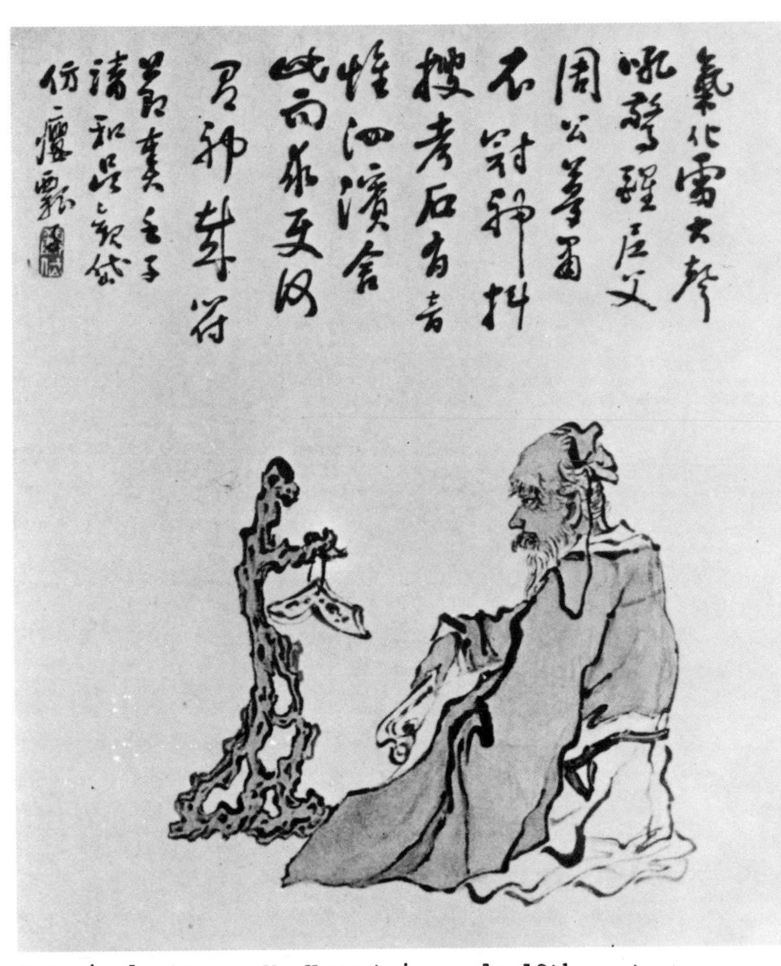

A musical stone. Wu Kwan-tai, early 19th century.

THE STORY OF THE CH'IN

A Friend from Afar

Wei Ying Wu

A friend who lives far, far away
Has sent me a gift of a fine zither.
This is his way of defeating distance
To give me some news about him:
"I am cold, untarnished as usual;
I have some good scholars for friends.
The strings for reminding you of the Way;
The lacquer for cementing our happy friendship."

THE STORY OF THE CH'IN

"Ch'in is Chin" so says *Pai Hu T'ung Yi,* an important historical reference written in the Han Dynasty, (2nd century B.C. – 3rd century A.D.). If this statement is too enigmatic and makes little sense, let it be explained that it is a play on the word "*Ch'in*" (琴) and "*Chin*" (禁) which are homonymns of different inflexions, meaning "zither" and "inhibition". The zither, so claimed the ancient Chinese, was an instrument that "inhibits wanton thoughts and puts the mind of the people right." That the *Ch'in* survives the turmoils and vicissitudes of Chinese history for more than two thousand years perhaps owes much to this statement, since it stands for "purity" in Chinese music as opposed to the "impurities" of alien musical influences. Moreover, it is said that Confucius himself played the *Ch'in* and the folk songs he collected in *Shih Ching* (Book of Songs) were actually zither tunes.

The *Ch'in* is, first of all, an indigenous musical instrument, different from those attributed to the nomadic tribes that roamed the northern Chinese plains in ancient times, or those imported from Central Asian countries during the Han and T'ang periods.

For the Chinese gentry, the *Ch'in* was a "virtuous" instrument, the playing of which was to be cultivated as a literary pastime and for spiritual elevation, and not to be compared to the playing of other folk instruments relegated to the lowly entertainer. Strict proscriptions were laid down for its playing. For example; it was not to be played unless one was properly "capped and gowned"; it was not to be played before a "vulgar" person. This reminds us of the practice in modern times when white tie and tails are almost *de rigueur* for the concert artist on a formal occasion, although in this age of commercial management, how the "vulgar" persons are to be excluded from the audience presents a problem.

A scholar playing the zither. Section of a painting by T'ang Yin (1470-1524).

The Formal *Ch'in* Player. Emperor Hui Tsung, Sung Dynasty ▶

In this arcadian setting, an elegant gentleman, formally attired, plays for two friends, cognoscenti of the *Ch'in* – one of them, head slightly bowed in a meditative mood and the other, looking up and ahead, perhaps at some distant hills. The air is filled with the delicate music of the zither, wafted by a gentle breeze.

The *Ch'in* used to be played on the lap of the player. Here, however, the player sits on a stool beside a table on which the instrument rests.

The "uncovered" *Ch'in* player

The Five "Don'ts":

Don't play in stormy weather
Don't play in a noisy market place
Don't play for a vulgar person
Don't play without sitting down
Don't play unless covered and gowned

The gentleman in the picture seems to have neglected one of the important proscriptions.

An aura of romanticism surrounds the *Ch'in*. Although its construction and tonal capacity suggest that the instrument is intended to be played indoors, it is often seen in Chinese scrolls as the inseparable companion of a scholar-poet in a majestic setting of mountains and streams. This identity with nature is quite understandable, considering that the wood of which the *Ch'in* is made is from the Wut'ung (*paulownia tomentosa*), a tree to be found "leaning against the steep precipice, tall and forboding and yet leafy and shady, a tree blessed with the harmonious essence of Heaven and Earth and imbued with the radiance of the sun and the moon."(7)

The legend goes that Yü Po-ya, a great *Ch'in* player, after failing to learn anything from his teacher the master Cheng Lien, was abandoned by him on the shore of a fairy island, where he meditated in solitude and learnt from nature and eventually becoming the "greatest" performer on the instrument. The story goes on to say that the innermost thoughts and feelings of Yü Po-ya were so deeply appreciated by his friend Chung Tzu-ch'i; as he listened to his playing, that when Tzu-ch'i died, Po-ya destroyed his instrument, swearing never to play it again, as there would never be anyone who could properly appreciate his music. Hence the term "*Chih Yin*" (music appreciated) came to be synonymous with "true friendship" in Chinese literary usage, the perfect communication of feelings not to be expressed in words. The above story of Yü Po-ya and Chung Tzu-ch'i was probably read out of its musical context, for the famous

Playing music in a majestic setting. The fisherman joins the audience. Chu Te-jun, 1294 - 1365.

林下鳴琴

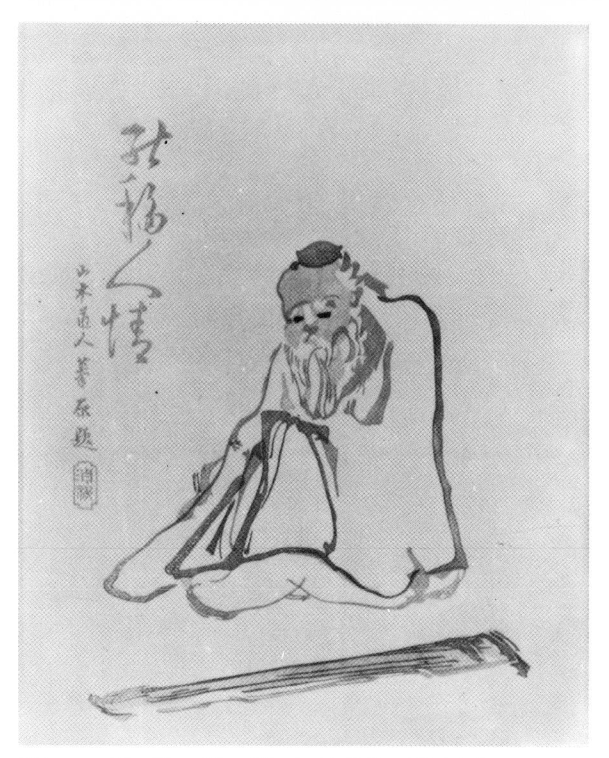

Old man with zither. Woodblock print after Huang Shen

The Forsaken Ch'in

Po Chü-i

Made of silk strings and the wood of wu-t'ung,
The ch'in *pours forth the sound of antiquity.*
Bland and insipid? The sound of antiquity
Appeals not to the modern ear.
Its jade studs lack not lustre though long disused,
On its red strings dust and dirt have gathered.
For a long time it has been abandoned
But its clear sound lingers in the air.
For you I wouldn't refuse to play, 'tis true,
But who else amongst us would care to listen!
What have made it so, degraded it so?
The barbaric oboe and the jangling Cheng.

compositions of Po-ya are lost forever. But music that is close to nature is not wanting in the music for the *Ch'in*. Listen to the following tune (play it on any instrument or just hum it) from an ancient tablature, the "Three Refrains of the Theme of Plum Blossoms", and hold your breath at the plum blossom falls softly on the ground:

Excerpt from *Mei Hua San Lung* (Three variations of the Theme 'Plum Blossoms')(8)

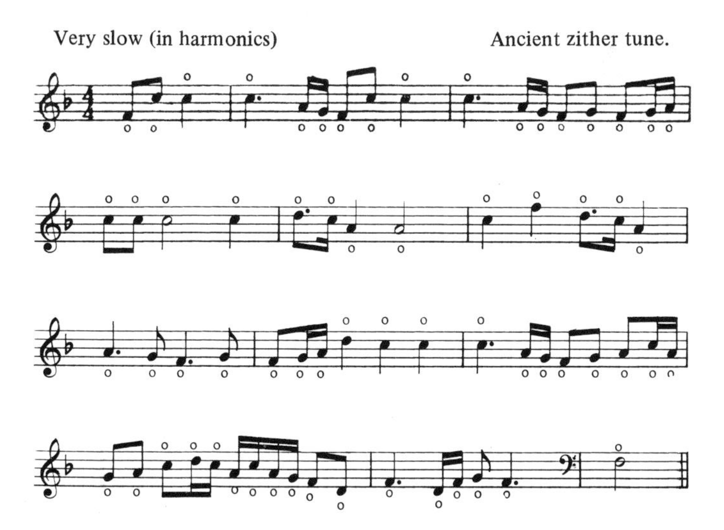

Not all the feelings expressed by the *Ch'in* are of such spiritual nature, however. The *Ch'in* was used also to evoke the passion of the flesh as for example, in the romantic story of Szuma Hsiang-ju who wooed and won the lovely young widow Cho Wenchun. The music of *Kuang Ling San*, an epic piece of music about the assassination of the tyrant king of Han by Nieh Chen was attributed to Hsi K'ang, a rebel and poet, who was also a great master of the *Ch'in*. While playing the *Ch'in* late in the night, so the story goes, Hsi K'ang was visited by a spirit on whose inspiration he composed this famous piece, reminding us of Tartini and his "Devil's Trills" sonata. But let us not indulge in these stories and return to the instrument itself.

The idea of "silk attached to wood" for making an instrument must have occurred to the ancient Chinese in very early time, and the invention was attributed to Fu Hsi, one of the five legendary emperors who is supposed to have lived in the third millenium B.C. An early ideograph has [ideograph] for the word 樂 (music) in oracle bone inscription, which was thought to indicate the idea of attaching cords of silk 𢆶 to a piece of wood (木). The Chinese characters for the *Ch'in* and the *Sê* both share the same radical 玨 which suggests instruments with cords stretched over a series of frets. The use of a wooden surface with a resonant box over which strings are stretched is certainly unique among early musical instruments. In Mesopotamian culture, the earliest string instrument, the *zagsal*, the Assyrian harp, has strings mounted on a frame. The Chinese *Ch'in*, with strings mounted on a resonant box, seems to be older than other instruments of

Hsi K'ang, one of the Seven Sages of the Bamboo Grove, was reputed to be a virtuoso of the *Ch'in*. Woodblock print.

this type. An instrument with seven strings stretched over a resonant box approximately 4.5 feet long and 6 inches wide, its entire surface being used as the finger board, the *Ch'in* must be considered *sui generis* among the psaltery group of instruments since it has no frets to predetermine the pitch; the strings are stopped by the player's fingers, and indeed the entire tonal system can be altered at will. The invention of the *Hui*, a series of studs of mother-of-pearl along the side of the finger board marking the harmonic stops on the strings, is particularly significant since it seems to show that as early as 2000 years ago, an important acoustic principle was understood by the Chinese. The *Ch'in* had by this time already become a versatile musical instrument with a wide range of more than four octaves and the capacity to produce a variety of tonal effects.

Szuma Hsiang-ju, a poor but talented scholar serenading the young widow Cho Wen-chün who listens stealthily behind the screen with her maid. Wen-chün's father and a guest sat in rapt attention. It was Wang Chi (the guest) who had arranged the meeting. One may guess that the figure in the foreground is Wang Chi who has the satisfaction of seeing that the meeting is bearing fruit. ▶

A gambling chit with the designation of twenty thousand coins.

There was the story of a fine scholar using music to woo his lady-love. Szuma Hsiang-ju was much attracted by the beauty of a widow, Cho Wen-Chün who lived with her rich father after her husband's death. Traditional morals frowned upon re-marriage, and courtship in the present case had to be done in a most subtle manner. Szuma chose to play on his zither a melody called "A phoenix seeking his mate."

The phoenix has returned to his native town
Having been abroad seeking his mate.
When time is not in his favour what could he do?
But tonight he will be received in a grand mansion.
There in an inner chamber a beauteous maid resides;
But how far she seems to be, how tantalizing!
Oh to be mandarin-ducks, our necks entwining,
Flying together up and down in the blue sky!

The making of this instrument was an art worthy of the great Italian luthiers. It was said that Tsai Yung, a great maker of the *Ch'in*, used to search the forests for burnt wood, the dry crackle of burning wood being an indication that the wood was of superior tonal quality. The *Ch'in* is prized for its age and specimens from the *T'ang* and *Sung* periods, which are supposed to emit the sound of "gold and jade", are priceless treasures. With its pure lines and elegant shape, the *Ch'in*, carved from a piece of old wood, shimmering in the subdued glow of ancient lacquer and decorated with autographs of famous people is indeed an object of great beauty.

Since the *Ch'in* is the instrument of the gentry, its music should be peaceful and harmonious, devoid of stress and excitement. The ideal tonal qualities – pure, delicate, pale and faint – are to be sought after. The sound of the instrument is sometimes imagined rather than heard as when a stopped string is struck and the finger of the left hand glides along the strings with various motions in a lingering diminuendo until the sound becomes almost inaudible. Poets even sing of a "stringless *Ch'in*", imagining it as echoing the music of the heavens.

The possibilities of the *Ch'in* as a musical instrument were probably recognized quite early by people who seriously practised it. They saw it as a vehicle for emotional expression and they exploited its capabilities. Music for the *Ch'in* expressed deeply-felt human feelings as in *Hu Chia Shih Pa P'ai* (Eighteen Stanzas from the Music of the Hun's Horn) which describes the longings of an exiled princess for her homeland, or as in *Chiu K'uang*

(Drunken Rage) which expresses the anger of a drunken poet protesting against some social injustice. Music that went against the injunctions of the *Ch'in* was frowned upon, and the battle was not won without a struggle. For example, *Kuang Ling San* (mentioned above), a piece of music embodying the most profound technique and musical expressions of which the *Ch'in* is capable, was hailed as the "greatest" *Ch'in* piece of all times, but it was also blamed for its "murderous" sound and for the "crude" excitement it created which was thought to be at variance with the nature of the instrument. It was, incidentally, condemned for grossly insulting the ruler, since the second lowest string representing the "subject" is tuned to the same pitch as the first string representing the "ruler", thus placing the two on an equal footing!

Let us compare the characters of these two schools of the *Ch'in* with the following musical examples:

A. Ode to the Ch'in(9)

B. Excepts from Kuang Ling San(10) (attributed to Hsi K'ang)

Another example showing the versatility of this instrument is taken from a tablature of 1876 "Cascading Waters"(11) by *Chang Kung-shan* of the Szechuan School, an example of "nature music" in the *Ch'in* repertoire:

The above musical examples transcribed into Western staff notation convey little of the actual effect of the music as played on the *Ch'in*. These examples rather suggest a general rhythmic pattern and the tempi of the music, but the ever-changing timbre of the sound produced by the fingernails and the fleshy part of the finger, by the relative strength implied in the alternate use of the thumb, the forefinger, the middle and the fourth fingers in striking the string, and the degree of pressure exerted by the fingers of the left hand to achieve the desired effects can only be appreciated when the instrument is played by a master.

Assasination of the Prince of Han. Rubbing from a bas-relief, Han Dynasty (3rd Century B.C.)

The bas-relief depicts the assasination of the Prince of Han by Nieh Cheng. The story became the theme of *Kuang Ling San*, attributed to Hsi K'ang.

Nieh Cheng's father was killed by the Prince of Han for failing to deliver on time a sword which he was commissioned to make. For ten years Nieh Cheng learned to play the zither until he became an incomparable virtuouso. The Prince of Han was an avid lover of the zither and when he heard about such a fine player, he summoned him to perform in his presence, not realizing the hidden intention of Nieh. So while the Prince was intent upon listening to the zither, sitting close of the player, Nieh pulled out a dagger from the instrument, stabbed and killed him instantly.

Fearing lest his identity might endanger his mother, he mutilated his face beyond recognition and killed himself.

A large sum was offered by the Court for information leading to the identification of the murderer. To perpetuate the fame of her son, Nieh's mother sat beside his corpse and killed herself, thus identifying it.

Music for the *Ch'in* ranges from short pieces played alone or as accompaniment to singing, to large works consisting of many sections. A large *Ch'in* piece is in free form, something like a fantasia in Western music. It begins with an introduction in free rhythm with indefinite tonality. The main themes appear in the section that follows, in which the rhythm and the tonality are established. This is followed by a section of development with contrasting figures, justaposition and interplay. The tempo quickens as the music approaches the climax. This leads to a relaxation and lessening of the tension of the music. In this new section, shifting of tonal centers occurs and the themes are usually repeated. A coda in "*stretto*" closes the piece with a series of harmonics.

Unlike music for entertainment, which was left to the humbler practioners to pass on to posterity by word of mouth, music for the *Ch'in* is codified. Beginning with a system which describes in words how a passage is to be played, it has evolved into a unique system of notation using a series of complexes consisting of numerals and strokes from Chinese characters. One complex indicates fingeings, the order of the strings, positions to be stopped, the sequence of notes, and the effects called for.

The following example(12) gives an idea of how the complex system works.

To play  , the complex [illegible] may be used. In this complex, 龷 is a radical of the character 散, meaning in this context "open" (open string). 六 is a numeral for six and 乚 is a stroke from the character 挑, meaning outward plucking by the forefinger. The hand position for this complex is:

The same note may be played differently as indicated by another complex 尸六. Here 尸 is a radical of the character 擘 meaning inward plucking by the thumb, and 六 is the numeral, the sixth string to be played. The hand position for this is:

Even without hearing the note as it is played in different ways, one can imagine the subtlety of the tone as it is produced with different degrees of strength and agility implied in the inward and outward motions of the forefinger and the thumb. As a further illustration, the musical figure

is represented by the complexes of 蠶, 㚏. The player stops the fourth string at the position of the ninth "hui" (a stud indicating the position where the string is stopped) with the thumb of the left hand, plucks the string with the right middle finger in outward motion, then moves the left thumb up one position (one whole tone) and quickly returns to the original position, before the player again plucks the string with the right middle finger in an inward motion. The result will be a solid tone on D, a lingering tone on E and again a solid tone on

D. The nuances and subtleties of the timbre when the instrument is played by a master are sometimes compared to the spectrum of colour gradations in a fine water-and-ink Chinese painting.

The following passage(13) transcribed from a piece of music for the *Ch'in* shows both the descriptive and the complex systems of notation side by side with the Western staff notation:

Although the complex system of notation is by far the most comprehensive of the Chinese notation systems, it gives no indication on the meter of the music. Certain rhythmic and metric factors are implied in a complex, much as rhythm is often implied in the harmony of Western music. In the so-called vocal school where the *Ch'in* accompanies singing, the music follows the natural cadence of a stanza as in the chanting of a poem. But in instrumental music, the note value is left to the player to interprete. Thus, one and the same piece of music from a tablature may have several different versions according to the interpretation of the schools of playing. A tablature then must go through the process of reconstruction and re-creation before it becomes music.

During the Ming and Ch'ing dynasties, it became fashionable for the literati to commit the music and literature for the *Ch'in* to large block printing with such titles as "The Wondrous Secret Tablatures of the Gaunt Hermit" or "Heritage of Tunes from the Remote Past", so that together with hand-copied manuscripts and examples from other sources, some 150 volumes comprising about 3000 pieces of music in tablature have been handed down.

It should be noted that this is the only type of music which has been handed down in large quantities in a comprehensive notation system. Throughout its existence in more than two thousand years, the instrument has passed often from the dilettantes to the hands of the entertainers and the professional musicians. In the course of time, its music must have absorbed elements of both the classical and folk traditions. The rich legacy of music for the *Ch'in* is therefore an important source for the study of Chinese music and its development.

臞仙神奇秘譜 下卷

霞外神品

黄鍾調 外無射

神品無射意

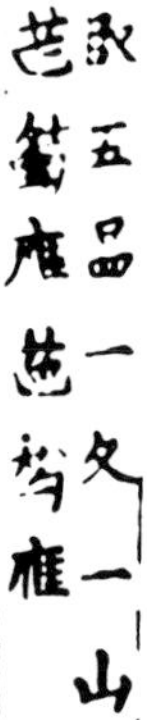

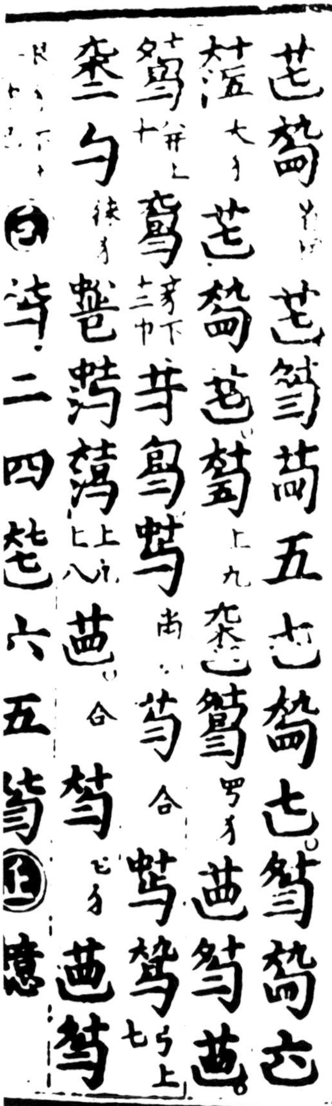

Ch'in **Tablature** A page from the "*Wondrous Secret Tablature of the Gaunt Hermit: Superior Specimens from Beyond the Evening Clouds.*"

The fanciful title might have been made up by the man (with the pseudonym of the Gaunt Hermit) who committed the complexes of the *Ch'in* to large block printing. It was fashionable for the literati during the Ming Dynasty to print the *Ch'in* tablatures of which some 150 volumes are known to exist.

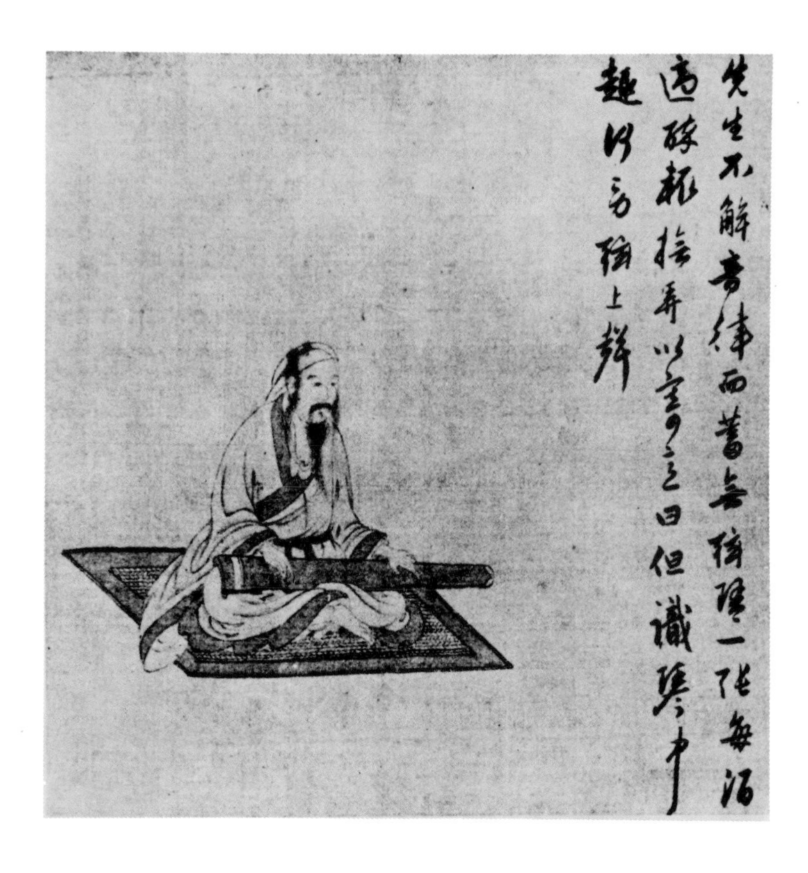

T'ao Ch'ien was not conversant with the principles of music. He kept a zither which had no strings on it. When he got himself wine-rapt, which he often did, he would pretend to play it. He used to say: "To know the pleasures of the zither is enjoyable enough. Why must one depend on the strings for the music.?"

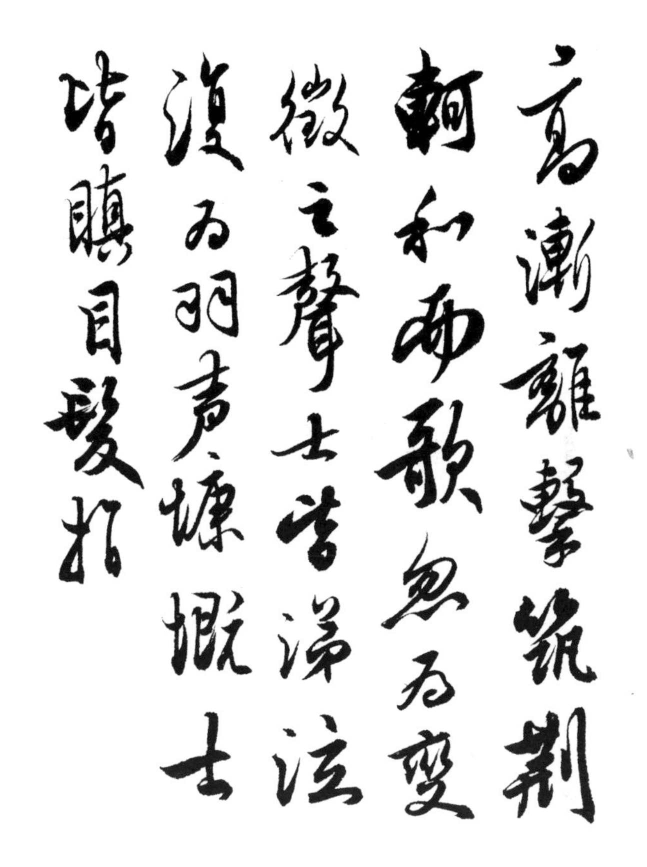

Kao Chien Li played his bowed zither while Ching Ko sang. A sudden change of the music to the Pien Chih *mode brought tears to all who were present. When the music changed again to the* yü *mode, all were filled with a great sense of indignation and hatred.*

Pien Chih is the raised fourth in the heptatonic scale, and the sudden departure from the original key may have an eerie effect. Yü is the fifth mode of the pentatonic scale, having the quality of a minor mode.

Ch'in Playing in a Natural Setting. After Lo Hung, T'ang Dynasty.

Communion with nature more than anything else is the object of the musician.

The Ch'in

Li Po

A monk of Szechuan has arrived with his ch'in
From the holy O-Mei Mountain in the West.
For me he plays the instrument and the sound
Evokes singing pines from caverns numberless.
Like running water, it cleanses the listener's mind;
Its falling cadence mingles with the bells in winter.
I am unaware that evening has come upon us
As the autumn clouds thickening darken the blue hills.

A Thirteenth Century *Sung Ch'in* ▶

This famous zither bears the title "*Hai Yueh Ch'ing Hui*" (Clear Light of the Rising Moon from the Sea). Choiceness of wood, fine lacquering and elegant shape are the attributes of this splendid specimen. Along both sides of the sound trough on the back of the instrument are inscriptions of famous people. The sound it produces is described as having the quality of gold and jade.

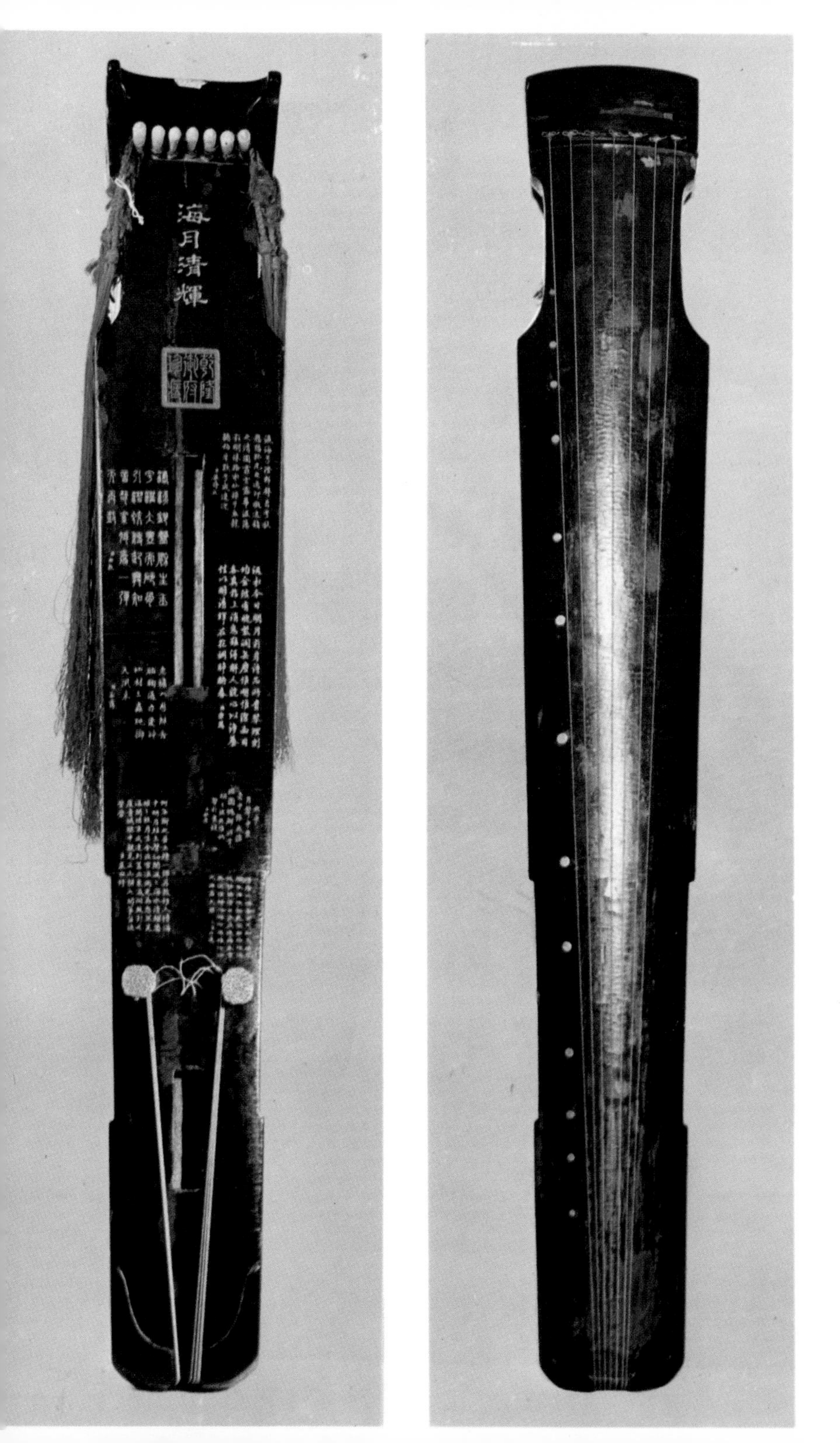
海月清輝

Dead antelope in the Field

In the field an antelope lies dead
Wrapped up in a mat of white;
A maiden comes with thoughts of spring
And a fop eyes her with amorous intent.

In the forest grow oaks short and stout,
In the field a deer lies dead
Tightly bound with a matting of white rushes.
Like a jewel a maiden appears.

"Behave yourself and get along.
My handkerchief please do not touch;
Make not my dog bark."

(from Book of Songs)

The songs on this and the opposite page are about love between man and woman. As such they are scornfully dismissed as songs "sung behind the mulberry hedges." However, these folk songs are said to have been collected by Confucius himself.

Sweet Maid

O sweet maiden, fair and demure –
At the wall corner we were to meet.
Since she did not appear
Scratching my head I knew not what to do.

My handsome maiden, gentle and coy –
A slender red reed she did give me.
O, the brightness of the red reed
Is not comparable to her beauty.

She brought back a spray of T'i
So fine and rare a gift.
Oh, it's not the spray I treasure –
But it is a gift from her.

(from Book of Songs)

Po Ya studied the zither under Master Cheng Lien for three years without being able to accomplish "solitude of the spirit and a oneness of feelings." Cheng Lien said to him, "My teacher Fang Tzu Chun is living in the Eastern sea. He has the power of changing a person's dispositions." So he took Po Ya with him to visit his teacher. When they arrived at Peng Lai, the Land of Immortals, he bade Po Ya stay and practise the zither while he went to meet his teacher. So he set off in a boat and for ten days was not heard of. Po Ya, left alone, heard only the sound of the waters surging and breaking against the shores, of the solitude of the forest and the wailing of birds. He sighed, feeling enlightened, and said, "This is how my teacher tries to change my dispositions." He sang to the accompaniment of his zither and achieved in a short time what he had so long striven for. When Cheng Lien returned, Po Ya welcomed him back in a boat. He became an accomplished player, unsurpassed in the kingdom.

Ts'ai Yung was extremely sensitive to the subtleties of sound. Once someone was burning a large log from a Wu-t'ung tree. The crackling sound intrigued Ts'ai and he immediately caused the burning to be stopped and had the log made into a zither. One end of the instrument was still charred when finished. It proved to be a zither that produced a

beautiful sound. On another occasion, Ts'ai was invited to dinner. Upon entering the hall of his host, he heard zither music from which his sensitive ears detected murderous intent. So he immediately beat a retreat and went home.

When the host heard about this, he went to see Ts'ai, who told him what happened. The zither player, who was not the host, explained: "While playing the zither I was witnessing a drama between a mantis and a cicada. The latter was making as if to take flight and I was anxious lest the mantis unwittingly let it escape. My music must have reflected this aggressive anxiety."

Someone presented the Prince of Chu with a zither which yields an exquisite sound "that for days went round and round the palace pillar". The Prince was delighted and indulged so much in listening to the sound that he neglected state affairs. A concubine name Fan said to him: "Sir, please forgive me for saying that you are being over-indulgent. In ancient times, King Chieh lost his life owing to an excessive fondness for the music played by Mui Shih; King Ch'ou lost his kingdom owing to his weakness for effeminate music. Now your Highness has not attended Court for seven days, spell-bound by the sound of the zither. Do you want to follow the footsteps of those kings?"

The Prince forthwith took a metal sceptre and broke up the zither.

Who Cares to Listen to the Blind Old man?
Su Liu-peng (circa 1800)

The blind old man plucks the zither (*cheng*) with his right hand and plays a pair of clappers with his left.

The Inscription:

He may go on singing!
He may go on playing –
But where to find someone who appreciates.
Who cares if his voice be hoarse
Or his fingers cracked.
For the neighbour's girl just come of age
Sings with a voice sweet and tender.
What fool would listen to a blind old man!

Song of the P'i-P'a. Chin Nung.

The guardian of the East playing the *P'i-P'a* . Detail from a relief on the Chu-yung-kuan gate, near Peking, dated 1342.

THE STORY OF THE P'I-P'A

Next to the *Ch'in*, the *P'i-P'a*, a short lute[14], is the second most important Chinese musical instrument. Unlike the *Ch'in*, the instrument of the gentry, guardian of the "pure" musical tradition, the *P'i-P'a* is the instrument of the entertainer. As such, the *P'i-P'a* lacks the kind of mystical aura that surrounds the *Ch'in*, nor is there a philosophical basis for its *raison d'etre.* It was a "vulgar" instrument that no gentleman-scholar deigned to touch, and the cultivation of the art of playing this instrument and other "non-Chinese" musical instruments was not accepted as one of the "six arts". Music-making that deviates from the strict tenets of *Ya Yueh* – in other words, music that appeals to the senses – was often scornfully dismissed as something of "the like of *P'i-P'a* and *Chieh Ku* (a large drum)".

The *P'i-P'a*, as the generic name of all instruments plucked by the hand, was known to exist in China long before the instrument in its present form was introduced into the country around the fifth century. During the reign of Shih Huang T'i of the *Ch'in* Dynasty in the third century, B.C., the northern plains of China were frequented by Asiatic nomads, collectively known as the *Hu*, so that a great wall was built as a defence against these plundering hordes . While the court was busily warding off the invaders by dispatching troops to the north, it appears that the people in the border regions had mingled freely with these "barbarians" and had adopted some of their ways of life, especially in music and dancing, so much so that their instruments – the *P'i-P'a, Ch'iang Ti* (short oboe) and *Chieh Ku* –were popularly played by the Han people, becoming at the same time a part of the musical life of the defenders. The so-called Music of the Rampart so frequently alluded to in Chinese poetry must have retained strong elements of the music of the Hus. The prevailing mood that this music inspired was profound nostalgia, sadness of separation and the indulgence in the pleasure of the moment, that of drinking and dancing. The following lines of Li Chi aptly sum up the spirit of this music:

At fifteen, our maiden of Liaotung
Plays the *p'i-p'a* and excels in song and dance;
When from her oboe spins forth a frontier tune
Behold, the soldiers all are moved to tears.

Woman Player of P'i-P'a. From "*An Evening of Entertainment with Han Hsi-tsai*" by Ku Hung-chung

This is the central portion of the famous painting by Ku Hung-chung (ca. 950). Han Hsi-tsai, a high official in the Southern T'ang Dynasty was known for his lavish living. To find out how he entertained his guests, the Emperor dispatched his court painter Ku Hung-chung to Han's house, disguised as a guest and to make sketches of what took place during an evening of entertainment. Judging from the size of the *P'i-P'a* and the absence of any body frets below its short neck, it may be an instrument with a rather low register.

Detail of the *P'i-P'a* player overleaf.

The word *P'i-P'a* brings to mind many tragic-romantic stories of this period of Chinese history. There is the story of the Lady Chao Chün, the beautiful and talented court lady who was ordered to marry Hsien Yü, the Khan of the Huns who came to the Chinese court to seek the hand of a Han noblewoman for his queen. Dressed in full military regalia, Chao Chün took along a *P'i-P'a* and rode out of the rampart into the wilderness. This, of course, was a much resorted to means of appeasing the barbarians, and so a similar story was told by Fu Hsüan in the preface of his famous poetic essay *P'i-P'a Fu* (Ode to the P'i-P'a) that "the *P'i-P'a* was not known in history, but an old sage gave this account: the Emperor of Han sent a noble princess to marry King Kumi of the Wu-suns. Mindful of her longing for home during her journey, he ordered a craftsman to cut down a traditional instrument to make one for playing on horseback." Then attaching some mystical significance to a musical instrument, Fu Hsüan went on, "considering this new instrument: its being hollow within and solid without symbolizes heaven and earth; its round body and straight neck the *Yin* and the *Yang*; its twelve *Chus* (ledges) correspond to the system of *Lü Lü*; its four strings figure the four seasons. Its name *P'i-P'a* is borrowed from some alien dialect and it is so called that it may be readily accepted in foreign countries". It appears then that a foreign instrument known as *P'i-P'a* had existed at that time, and that the Chinese made a native version to match it.

Jade Flute, Ho Tzu, contemporary. The inscription is a poem by Li Po. Page 8 has the same poem in formal script and the translation.

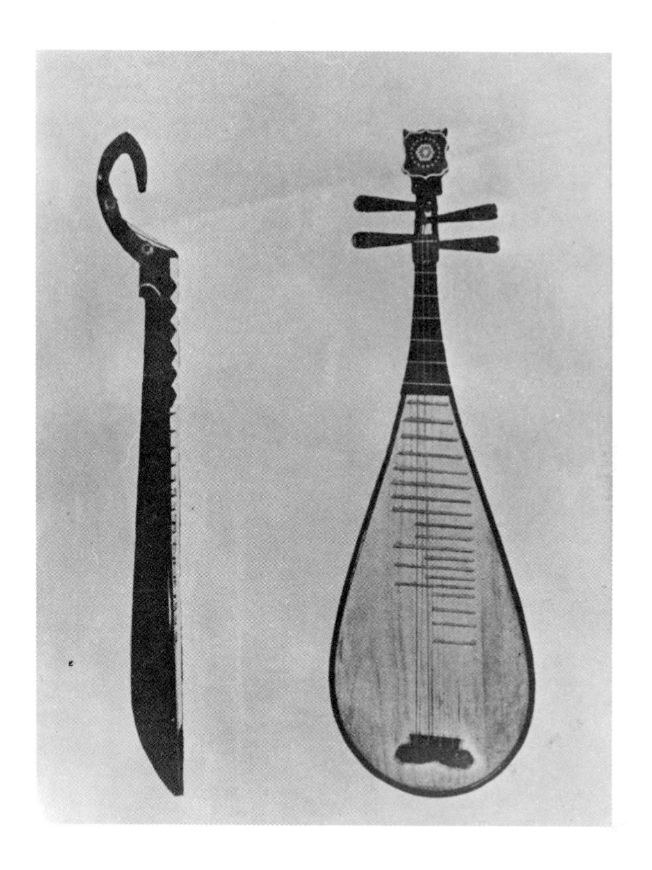

P'i-P'a (modern version)

The modern *P'i-P'a* differs from the T'ang *P'i-P'a* in several aspects: its body is tapered to a pear shape; it has many more ledges and frets (6 ledges and 19 body frets) and the protective body band is done away with. The modern player holds the instrument upright and reaches down with his left hand to play in the high positions. He has discarded the plectrum in favour of the bare fingers (with nails) to play the strings. The Japanese *Biwa*, on the other hand, retains the form and other features of its prototype, the T'ang *P'i-P'a*.

Buddhist Angel Musicians. From a mural in Tun Huang

Although a group like this one is often seen with instruments of mixed origins, the musicians here have only indigenous Chinese instruments.

As the word *P'i-P'a* was said to be of foreign origin, some clues may be found in other ancient languages for similar-sounding words. *Bharby* in Sanskrit means "striking the strings"; *Barbyton* in ancient Greek refers to a lute-type instrument, and so is *barbot*, an instrument closely resembling the Chinese *P'i-P'a* and is seen on the silver urns of the Sassanian Dynasty of ancient Persia. The word *P'i-P'a* 琵琶 in Chinese is onomatopoetic, and as explained in *Shih Ming* (Explanation of Terms) "*P'i* is the forward motion of the hand pushing the string, and *P'a* the backward plucking motion." Hence, the word came to refer to all instruments plucked by the hand.

The ovoid *P'i-P'a* with the peg-box bent backwards was said to be of Turco-Iranian origin and was brought to China via the old city of *Kucha*, Sinkiang, which stood in the great trade route north of the *T'ien Shan* range. It came with foreign envoys to pay homage to the Chinese court with rare gifts and the usual entourage of musicians, dancers, jugglers and courtesans for the harem of the Han rulers. It was indeed a trend in reverse from former days when the Han court used to send Chinese noblewomen to appease the *Hus*. Thus music made its way from Central Asia to the Middle Kingdom and its impact is felt as keenly today as it was then. Musicians who came to China via the great trade routes including famous *P'i-P'a* players were mostly natives of Kashgar, Samarkand and Bukhara in the region that was historically known as Turkestan, and they brought along a host of foreign instruments such as the angular harp, short oboes, tabla, frame and cylindrical drums and metallophones. These instruments were placed alongside traditional Chinese musical instruments to form orchestras to perform the musics of different countries. It also appears that the *P'i-P'a* came with the incursion of Buddhism at about the same time, for this instrument with its player, sometimes in the person of the Apsara, is commonly seen in cave paintings and stone carvings in such important centres of Buddhist relics as the Caves of the Thousand Buddhas in Tun Huang, the caves in Mai Chi Shan and in Yun Kang. *Su Chih-p'o* (*Sujiva* in Sanskrit), a legendary virtuoso of the *P'i-P'a* who, escorting a Turkic queen to China in the year 568 introduced the "seven modes" from India which, it was said, correspond to the Chinese modes. All of this is evidence that both Islamic and Indian cultures had converged on the road to China.

Although it is not known exactly who first brought this instrument to China, the historical background of its appearance on the Chinese musical scene is worthy of attention.

Beginning from early fourth century, the Chinese rulers had been so weakened that they were unable to contain the so-called five nomadic tribes and were forced to establish themselves in the Yangtze valleys in the South. The whole of North China was soon overrun by the Hus, the barbarians, disintegrating into many regimes, one succeeding another. It was during this period of great upheavals that the intermingling of the races became widespread, with the Han people acquiring the manners and mores of the aliens.

The lively music of the Hus, or *Hu Yueh*, posed

a sharp contrast to the rather staid and inhibitive ritualistic music of the court, and was widely practised among the people. This, in turn, had a great impact on the court. Stories were told of decadent rulers who, conscious of their brief reigns, indulged in the pleasures of the flesh, which this new music inspired. By the time the country was again reunified, (Sui Dynasty, 586-619 followed by the prosperous reign of the T'ang rulers 619-907), the musical taste of the Chinese had become quite adapted to extrinsic musical values.

The popularity of *Hu Yueh*, in which the *P'i-P'a* played a leading role, was undoubtedly due to the vitality and richness of its music, particularly to its association with dancing. The so-called "new sound" was described as "stirring the soul of the listener and jarring his ears". Practitioners of this music, many of whom were aliens, adopted Chinese names and customs and gained access to the inner circle of the court, the most favoured ones becoming "mandarins", as music officials. Song and dance were the order of the day in the capital city of Ch'ang An. In this atmosphere, many court musicians like Li Kuei-nien and Wan Pao-ch'ang rose to prominent positions, keeping intimate company with their lords and masters in making music. Emperor Hsüan Tsung (ca. 713) of T'ang Dynasty was an accomplished musician and composer, and it was he who instituted the *Li Yuan* (Pear Garden), a school for entertainers placed under his personal supervision.

Bacchanalia of the Hus. After a painting by Hu Huai, Five Dynasties (907–960)

The scene depicts the King of the Hus and his beautiful Han wife Wen-chi, each with a set of attendants. There is music from a pair of *K'ung Hou* (harp), the rhythmic clapping of hands and the stomping of the dancer's boots. Wen-chi and her attendants were watching demurely, obviously reluctant to share in the fun.

黄一凤

When peonies were in bloom, Emperor Hsüan Tsung of T'ang invited the poet Li Po to his palace and commanded that he compose a song in praise of Yang Kuei Fei, the imperial concubine. The result was the famous Song of Pure Peace:

The fleecy clouds recall her dress
The flowers recall her face –
Spring whispers to the garden fence
of her departed grace.
Upon Jade-Mountain's scented path
If I chance not to meet her
Then surely at the Emerald Terrace
Under the moon I'll greet her.

Indulgence in Music and Dancing. Woodblock print 16th century

The Emperor Hsüan Tsung of T'ang Dynasty plays the hoop drum to accompany the dancing of his favourite concubine Kuei Fei, with Prince Ning on the Dragon-Head flute, while Ho Huai-chi, a court musician is seen playing a pair of clappers.

Works of music from foreign lands, however, were not readily accepted without modification. As soon as they came into contact with Chinese music, a process of sinicization set in, so that T'ang music became a mixture of Turco-Indian, Chinese and other elements. The famous *Ta Ch'ü,* a large musical form consisting of music, dancing and singing, was a melting pot of different musical trends. This process of assimilation and absorption of foreign musical influences was carried through to modern times and is characteristic of Chinese musical development.

The *P'i-P'a* as it was first introduced, seemed to have a much larger body, with four strings, a short neck and four neck ledges. Judging from its shape and construction, it must have been an instrument of lower register, possibly a bass instrument, since by holding it sideways, the player could not reach down to stop the strings in the high positions. The fact that the *P'i-P'a* was frequently mentioned along with the long drum and other percussion instruments in accompanying dancing, suggests that it was given to playing strongly rhythmic music. The T'ang *P'i-P'a* and its player, among other things, is magnificiently illustrated in the famous large scroll "Scenes from Night Entertainment of Han Hsi-tsai" by the painter Ku Hung-chung (ca. 910).

As the instrument became sinicized, it also underwent changes both in structure and in its playing technique. The body was tapered down to a pear shape, and frets had been affixed to the body to form a series with the neck ledges. The modern *P'i-P'a* has 4 neck ledges (*Hsiang*) and as many as twenty-three frets , making up a range of four and half octaves with chromatic intervals. The sideway position of holding the instrument was changed into the upright position, and the plectrum was discarded in favour of the bare fingers. The T'ang tradition of playing the *P'i-P'a* sideways with a plectrum is however still preserved in Korea and in Japan to this day. These changes prompted the rapid development of its playing technique. It became a solo instrument with a distinct personality and no longer confined only to accompanying dancing.

The lore of the *P'i-P'a* is as rich as it is fascinating. There is, for example, the legend of Kang K'un-lun, a renowned master of the *P'i-P'a* in the year *Cheng Yüan* (785) who lost a duel in *P'i-P'a* playing in a rain-praying festival to the monk Tuan Shan-pen disguised as a young girl, and had to give up playing for ten years to rid of his bad habits in order to relearn the art from the monk. The famous *P'i-P'a Hsing* (Song of the Lute of Po Chü-i), immortal poetry as it is, contains such a rich description of its playing technique that it has become a source of musical study.

Music for this instrument was not codified as that for the *Ch'in* was. Much of it was passed directly from the master to the pupil. What is handed down to us on paper is notated in a simple system of the *Kung Ch'e* alongside of which are marked special signs indicating certain fingerings and effects. Such simple notation conceals the elaborate technique in playing the instrument. A simple melody may be embellished with florid runs and doubling of the notes, and a bravura passage raises a storm with great clashing chords. Infinite tonal effects are achieved by resorting to the twisting and meshing of the strings and by playing in tremolo, vibrato and glissando, by the use of the nailed and the fleshy part of the fingers in plucking, and by hitting the sounding board!

Music for the *P'i-P'a* is almost all descriptive. Essentially folk music, many short pieces bear such titles as "Riding Backwards Astride the Donkey" or "The Little Nun turns her Thoughts to Springtime." Sometimes an ironical twist is implied in re-naming a piece, undoubtedly in an attempt to make it appear less "vulgar", as for example when the poetic title "White Snow in Sunny Springtime" is attached to a set of magnificent variations on a theme which in fact is a very popular ditty known as "The Little Bald-headed Monk". Like music for the *Ch'in*, music for the *P'i-P'a* goes by its schools of playing, each with its distinctive characteristics. The more lyrical "civil" school is popular in the South and the bravura style of playing is identified with the Northern "Military" school.

The following modern transcription of a page from a piece of music of the "Military" school "The Great Ambuscade" gives an idea how the sounds of a great battle are depicted:

Excerpt from the "Great Ambuscade"

The *P'i-P'a* today is one of the most popular of Chinese musical instruments, and is used in virtually every type of music, and indispensable to folk ballads and folk operas. True to its tradition, the *P'i-P'a* is frequently seen in the hands of the female entertainer, as in the *T'an Tz'u* ballad of Shanghai and in many forms of musical story-telling.

The *P'i-P'a* has played a unique role in the history of Asian music. It was an inter-cultural carrier of music and catalytic to the assimilation of foreign musical elements by the Chinese. It has preserved in its repertory certain important musical forms of the great T'ang period, notably the so-called "large pieces". Last but not least, it has inspired great poetry and literature so well loved by the Chinese and other peoples.

Kang K'un-lun was a P'i-P'a virtuoso in the heyday of the T'ang Dynasty. After a period of drought, the West City staged a "music contest" as part of a rain-praying campaign. Kang went up the Eastern Terrace and played the song "Green Waist", transposed to a new "yü" mode. He was quite sure none in the opposite team could beat him. When he had finished, a girl appeared on the Western Terrace with a P'i-P'a and said. "I can play this piece and can transpose it to the mode of "Feng Hsiang" as well." When she put her plectrum to the strings, a thunderous sound arose, to the wonder and enchantment of all who heard it. Kang was overwhelmed and begged to be taken as a student. The musician turned out to be Monk Shan Pen in disguise. The following morning, Emperor Te Tsung summoned the monk and ordered him to teach Kang his extraordinary art. "Please play me a piece," said the monk to Kang, who did as requested. "How impure is your technique!" was the monk's comment. Kang said, "Master, you have the clairvoyance of a god. I began studying music with a neighbour's daughter who taught me to play on one string; after that I had several other teachers."

The monk advised Kang not to touch any musical instrument for ten or more years until he had shaken off his habits and be ready to learn new things. The Emperor gave permission and Kang ultimately mastered the art of the P'i-P'a.

* * * * * * * * * * *

SONG OF THE LUTE

Po Chü-i

I was seeing a friend off at the river's bend
Where reeds and maples rustled in the autumn wind.
A farewell feast was laid out in the departing boat –
It was a pity to have no music while we drank!
Even wine brought no relief – sadly we were going to part
As the moon through the mist shone darkling on the water.

Suddenly a lute sounded in the shimmering bay
And host and guests, enchanted, strained their ears.
We tried to trace the source of sound, which was now mute.
"Hello, where are you?" We called – but no answer came.

We saw her alone in a moon-drenched boat;
We drew nearer, had fresh candles brought,
Replenished the wine, and started feasting anew.
"Would you join us, please? We'd love to hear you play."
We coaxed and urged, but she was slow to come.
At last she did, her lute half hiding her face.
She tuned it, and lightly plucked its strings.
Before the melody flowed, passion was fully felt.
From the four strings her deft fingers evoked
Feelings of a life full of frustrations and regret.
Then with eyes cast down, she hugged the instrument.

Lightly caressing, slowly stroking, she plucked and swept.
First playing the Rainbow Skirt, then the Six-measure Song.
The bold strings – they pattered like dashing rain.
The fine strings – they sounded like lovers' whispers.
Chattering and pattering, pattering and chattering –
As pearls, large and small, on a jade platter fall.
Like orioles heard under flowering bushes
Or a busy spring bubbling down a pebbled stream.
It froze. The sound ceased. An unspeakable sadness
Surfaced: now silence was sweeter than sound.
Then without warning the music swelled again,
Gushing forth – like water bursting from a broken vase,
Or the clashing of swords and spears of armoured knights.
With a flourish, all the strings sounded in a clashing chord.
Silence reigned. The boats around were quiet.
The moonlit sky was milky with the autumn mist.
With a sigh she put the plectrum between the strings,
Adjusted her dress and, having curtseyed, stood.

She spoke, "I was brought up in the capital.
At thirteen, I became an accomplished player.
I was endowed with unusual grace and charm.
Wealthy young men pressed suit with precious gifts;
My songs brought numberless rolls of silk.
Jade combs and hairpins – I broke them beating time;

Blood-red silk skirts – I spoiled them with wine stains.
It was a life of merriment and time slipped by.
My brother was posted to the frontier and my mother died,
And as I grew older, fewer admirers came.
At last, I met a merchant and bore his name.
He thought little of leaving home, more of his profits.
He's been gone a month now, buying tea,
Leaving me alone with the cold river and the moon.
Of my salad days I am wont to dream
Then weep and wake up with reddened eyes."

My heart ached to hear her plaintive songs,
I sighed as she slowly unfolded her story.
"Deserted creatures both, we are two of a kind –
Friends we are, though newly met – why should we mind?
Since I was banished from the capital last year
I have been an invalid here in Hsün-yang.
I live near a river where it's low and wet,
Reeds and bitter bamboos grow around my hut:
Cuckoos cry and gibbons wail by day and night.
Even the blossom of the flowers and the brightness of the moon
Do not suffice and I must drink alone to ease my pain.
Is it that no one sings, or plays the flute?
No, but there is so little that pleases the ear.
Thus to listen to you play the sweet lute tonight
Is like hearing angels sing their dulcet songs.
So please refuse us not the favour of an encore

And I will compose for you a song in return."
She stood still, moved by my earnest words;
Then started, this time at a faster pace
Urgent, mournful, not as heretofore.
All who heard her hid their faces and wept.
Who amongst those present wept the bitterest?
It was I – my blue gown was drenched with tears.

·f the Lute. Ch'iu Ying (Section of a long scroll.)

Eighteen Songs of a Nomad Horn

Lady Wen-chi, daughter of Ts'ai Yung, a statesman of the Han dynasty, was taken captive by the Huns who drove down from the northern frontier. She was made the wife of the commander-in-chief of the nomad tribe. For twelve years she lived with him, bearing him two sons. In eighteen stanzas she told about her feelings and tribulations: how unbearable the Huns were and how they stank, how she preferred death to marrying the chieftain; how sad the sound of the p'ip'a was in the deep of the night; how she wanted to communicate with her homeland without success; how when she bore her children she grew to love them in spite of her dislike of the land and its people.

When a ransom mission located her, the lady had to face the painful choice between remaining with her husband and children in the harsh and alien land that she detested or giving up the family and returning to her own homeland. Finally she opted for the latter.

* * * * * * * * * * *

A "Kucha" Orchestra

The immortals in flowing robes and headdresses play a variety musical of instruments of Islamic, Buddhist and Chinese provenance. From the fifth century onwards, Islamic and Buddhist influences from both the northern and southern routes of the Tienshan Range converged in China, making a strong impact on Chinese musical life. Kucha (now K'u Ch'e of Sinkiang Province), an old city in Turkestan, was the threshold where the Islamic musicians came with the envoys to pay homage to the Chinese court. However, a "Kucha" orchestra, in the T'ang tradition, not only comprises Islamic instruments like the lutes (*P'i-P'a*) but instruments of other origins as well.

歌者樂之聲也故絲不如竹竹不如肉善
歌者必先調其氣氤氳自臍出至喉乃
噫其辭即分抗墜之音既得其術可致
遏雲響谷之妙

愛立囑書
段安節樂府雜談
紀彭

Random Thoughts on th
Music of the *Yueh-Fu*

Tuan An Chieh (ca. 849)
(Calligraphy by Kee-pang MC
1885-1972

The essence of music-mal
in singing. That is why the so
silk is not as good as the so
bamboo, the human voice
superior to both. The com
singer must first regulate his b
ing, then force the air throu
diaphragm upwards until it r
the throat, whence issue the
conveyed in rising and
strains. Done to perfectio
music thus created would
berate in the ravines, causing
to stop moving as if spell-bou

WORDS AND MUSIC

The Musical Story-teller. Figurine unearthed from an ancient tomb of Western Han Dynasty (3rd century B.C.)

Musical story-telling, an ancient tradition which has survived to this day, is an art form from which blossoms a rich variety of folk ballads and music-dramas collectively known as *Chu Yi*, of which numerous types are still being performed in China. Vernacularism plays an important role in Chinese music and because of the subtle inflexions of the Chinese language and its many dialects, words and music are often intimately integrated.

WORDS AND MUSIC

The spoken word plays an important part in Chinese music. It is perhaps no exaggeration to say that no other country has a greater variety of music in which words and music are so intimately interrelated. To this body of music belong numerous types of musical story-telling, folk ballads, music dramas, folk operas and formal operas that are being performed and enjoyed by the people throughout the country. There is also the singing of *Ch'ü*, as *K'un Ch'ü*, poetry-singing in the *K'un Shan* dialect which is a phonetically-oriented and highly cultivated school of singing. Unlike the songs of the troubadours and minstrels which now belong to the past, except for an occasional revival, the various types of verbal-music are in every sense of the word the living music of China, not only because old classics are being revived but new contents are being constantly injected into old forms.

◀ **The Blind Musician**

Chiang Lien (ca. 1831)

Blind musicians often feature in Chinese folk lore. A blind girl singer accompanied by her blind parents – the trio used to roam the back alleys of Canton. They were also seen in tea houses, where they performed for a pittance. One of these figures was T'am S'am whose skill in doing a one-man show was legendary at the turn of the last century. T'am was said to have acquired his uncanny skill from a Taoist monk who imparted it to him as a reward for his filial piety. His skill was such that he could stage an entire operatic scene by singing various roles, while accompanying himself with percussion instruments, playing them simultaneously with his hands, feet and elbows. The instruments in the picture are identified as cymbals, gongs, hoop drum, clappers and the *Yüeh Ch'in* (moon guitar). A flute and a *sona* (oboe) are also seen lying on the mat, which he will pick up and play when not occupied with singing. In the end, T'am made a small fortune and was more than able to support his mother as a filial son should.

Blind musicians are credited with the creation of many important forms of folk music – the "Salt Water Tune", the "Dragon Boat Race Tune" and the soulful ballad "*G'ai Sum*", a kind of Cantonese *Fado*. They were once very popular among the Cantonese people. Unfortunately, due to long neglect, this important branch of folk music is in danger of being lost forever.

The art of articulating Chinese words especially in singing has been the subject of deep and intensive study by Chinese scholars past and present. This chapter does not propose to go into the complexities of the Chinese phonetic system, nor is it possible to do so in a few pages. Rather, the intention is to give the reader a brief idea of tonal inflexions of the words and their musical implications.

Tonal inflexions are not, of course, limited to the Chinese language. However, the Chinese language being monosyllabic with many homonyms, lends itself to great subtleties in inflexion. Two monosyllabic words such as *K'an* (homonym for read and cut) and *Shu* (homonym for book and tree) may either mean "read book" or "cut tree" according to the ways they are pronounced, and a simple phrase "*Jang Wo Wen Ni*" meaning "let me ask you" may land the inquirer in trouble, being misunderstood as "let me sniff you", if pronounced in the wrong tonal inflexions. Intelligibility therefore depends much on the inflexive pronunciation of the words, complicated by differences in local dialects.

Tonal inflexions not only imply pitch variations but pitch levels as well. Take, for example, the word "ma", a homonym for 麻 (adjective for dotted, pock-faced), 媽 (noun for mother, old lady), 罵 (verb for to chide) and 馬 (noun for horse). These homonyms representing four different words would be quite meaningless if pronounced on the same pitch level. If pronounced in the standard speech, *i.e.* Peking dialect in their proper inflexions, they would be understood as meaning "the pock-faced old lady chides the horse", as shown in the following diagram:

麻	媽	罵	馬
Ma	Ma	Ma	Ma
↗	—	↘	∨

The tonal inflexions shown in the above diagram may be regarded as pitch variations indicating an upward or downward shift or a curve in pitch. With some other dialects, however, definite pitch levels may be implied when these homonyms are pronounced. Pronounced in the Hunan (Changsha) dialect, the result would have the following intervals:

Pronounced in Cantonese, the intervals would be quite different:

It follows then, tonal inflexions of the words implying different pitch levels could make up a tune. This is the case of a popular Cantonese nursery song, the "Little Cockerel", whose musical intervals happen to coincide exactly with the pitch levels of the words as spoken:

This is not to be confused with the intoning in "poetry-chanting", although undoubtedly some relationship exists between the style of poetry-chanting and the more sophisticated *Ch'ü* singing with its strict adherence to phonetic articulation.

Some Chinese dialects such as the Szuchuan and Hunan dialects have their special pitch implications. The Szuchuan dialect has an upward swing and many a Szuchuan folk tunes follow this natural tendency as in the following folk song *Hsi Yi Shang* (Washing Clothes):

It is, of course, simplistic to suggest that the music of a particular region is governed strictly by the tonal inflexions of the words, although the particular mode of the music of a region is the result of musical usage which among other things, is influenced by the characteristics of the dialect of that particular region. Thus the minor third diphthong in the vowel of words pronounced in the Hunan dialect must account for the minorish character of the folk songs of that region. Similarly, the *Kao Chiang* (literally, high tune) style of Szuchuan opera appears to bear a certain relationship to the upward swing of the Szuchuan dialect; and the *Chui Tzu* ballad of Honan characterized by the frequent downward movement of a musical phrase relates to a certain style of speech, as in the following example:

From "*Ma Chien P'o Shui*"

etc.

In refined singing such as that in *Ch'ü* or in formal operas where music is not so straightforward as the simple folk tunes, much attention is still paid to the proper tone levels of the words to make them unmistakable to the listener. Close relationship between words and music characterizes all types of Chinese vocal music.

The vernacular tradition of Chinese music dates back to very ancient times. Chanting to the rhythmic accompaniment on a simple instrument is a form of entertainment common to many early cultures. In China, it has been kept alive as an important art form. The long history of the country, rich in ancedotes about the rise and fall of dynasties, in folk stories and romances familiar to every household, as well as heroic deeds in epic battles, is an inexhaustible source of musical material for the imaginative entertainer. This art form has proliferated into numerous types grouped under the generic term of *Shuo Ch'ang.*

Shuo Ch'ang (story-telling and singing) ranges from a single raconteur accompanying himself (or herself) on a long bamboo drum, a pair of clappers and a loop drum (in types such as *Yu Ku, Tao Ch'ing, Ta Ku* etc.) to a couple of entertainers man and woman (*Erh Jen T'ai*) or a small group of performs with melodic instruments like the P'i-P'a, San Hsien and the fiddle (in types such as *Chui Tzu Hsi, T'an Tz'u* etc.). Anecdotes from history or folk lore are recounted with great verve and elan by the talented performer. In a type like the *T'an Tz'u* ballad popular in Shanghai and Soochow, the singers by resorting to eye-movement, hand-gesture and a delicate turn of phrase could hold an audience spellbound for hours on end. The contents may be such romantic love stories as the Dream of the Red Chamber, the Story of the White Snake or the Pearl Pagoda. The music, often simple and improvised, provides the background to the recitation and serves to underline and highlight the climaxes of the story.

Shuo Ch'ang is a popular form of entertainment. In the old days, the performers, many of them blind, wandering from tea house to tea house or setting up a stand in some market square, earned a pitiable subsistence. Only in recent years has their position been elevated to that of the respectable artist enjoying the kind of esteem they deserve and are given the opportunity to entertain large audiences in the theatres.

With the establishment of urban centers, a more organized form of vocal music *Hsi Ch'ü* – music drama and opera – began to emerge. The evolution of the many types of opera is too complicated a process to describe here. Suffice it to point out that "Peking Opera" which many people consider the epitome of this art form, has its roots in the drama-songs of the Yüan and Ming Dynasties (13th to 17th centuries). Most significantly, the singing has become declamatory, having freed itself from the "word-note" formula, and "arias" have been developed. Yet, it remains strophic – different verses being set to the same tune, or a set of tunes. Although to the uninitiated, the music may sound sketchy, great artistry is required for the execution of a musical phrase, the success of which depends on the skilful accompaniment of the fiddle and the loop drum players. Percussion and other instruments are more of a supportive nature. Formal operas call into play acting, miming,acrobatics and colourful costumes, combined in a spectacular presentation.

Chinese vernacular music in its diverse forms provides a great variety of musical styles rich in local flavours. It is unfortunate that access to this living music is denied to many people including serious students of Chinese music who are not sufficiently versed in Chinese linguistics. Even among the Chinese, those from one part of the country would find it difficult to appreciate fully the music of another region.

The recent movement to standardize speech aiming at wiping out differences in pronunciation will undoubtedly adversely affect music with strong local flavour. It would be a great pity indeed to allow this living tradition of vernacular music to pass into oblivion.

Yung Hsin was a courtesan in the Court of Ming Huang of T'ang. One day the King gave a grand party and the guests, hundreds of them, made so much noise that the music and stage-show put on for the occasion was completely drowned by it. The Emperor was going to terminate the party when Kao Li-shih came up with an idea. Why not ask Yung Hsin to sing? So adjusting her hair, she began. Almost immediately, silence reigned supreme. Those who were happily disposed were filled with added zest; those sadly disposed were filled with unspeakable anguish.

Li Yen-nien was a fine musician in the court of Emperor Wu of Han. Once he sang this song in the presence of the Emperor:

In the North lives a beauty
Supreme and proudly aloof.
Her first glance is enough to destroy a city;
A second glance can subvert a kingdom.
Who does not know she is so devastating?
But such beauty is so rare!

The Emperor sighed and said: "A good song. But is there such a beauty in this world?" The Prince of Ping Yang said: "The younger sister of Li Yen-nien is such a beauty." And so she was presented and became the Emperor's favourite concubine. When she died, the Emperor was most distressed. A certain Ch'i Shao-weng claimed he was able to invoke the spirit of the dead. At the appointed hour, the Emperor awaited her arrival outside his chambers but was only able to see her spirit at a distance. The Emperor wrote a song:

Is it, or is it not
Her true dear self?
I stood and looked from a distance –
Why comes she so slowly, so late?

The court musicians were ordered to put this to music.

Musical Story-telling

P'ing T'an is an art form popular in Shanghai and Soochow. Performed in a tea house, two or three singers who represent the *dramatis personae* in a play, act out the story by relying on such gestures as *Yen Feng* (eye gesture) and *Shou Shih* (hand gesture), using sometimes their instruments and the fan as stage props. A favourite subject is secret love between a high-born maiden and the poor but brilliant young scholar as in the *Romance of the Western Chamber*. *P'ing T'an* begins with a short instrumental prelude, the *K'ai Pien*, introducing the singer who then proceeds *parlando* to give a synopsis of the story. The tunes follow the patterns set by the great masters. Instrumental accompaniment is mostly supportive. When exposed to this art form, the uninitiated will perhaps miss many fine points, but the *cognoscenti* will be enraptured by a deliberate accent in a dramatic moment, and relish every delicate turn of phrase sung in a dialect familiar to them from childhood.

Music appreciated. T'ang Yin, 1470 – 1524.

CONCLUSION

CONCLUSION

We have so far, with the help of illustrations, anecdotes and poetry, traced the progress of Chinese music over thousands of years. These pages must have revealed to the reader certain distinctive patterns in the history of Chinese music. Firstly, Chinese music is heterogeneous in origin, benefited by multi-ethnic influences not only within China herself but from countries far beyond her boundaries. Secondly, in this continuing process of cultural interaction, there has always been a strong trend to guard against alien musical influences and to preserve the so-called "purity" of Chinese music. Thirdly, foreign musics as soon as they were introduced into China were subjected to sinicization resulting in the amalgamation, through a slow but steady process of several hundred years, of foreign and native elements. One is also reminded that foreign musical influences were filtered through China to pass on eastward to Korea and Japan and southwards to the Indo-Chinese peninsula.

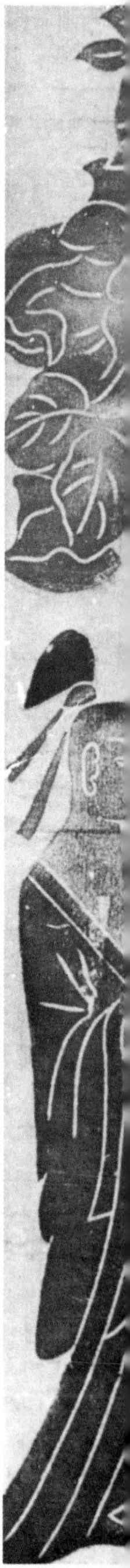

Musicians in Buddhist dress playing an assortment of Chinese instruments. From a mural in Tun Huang.

Students of Chinese history may be puzzled by the fact that these trends in Chinese music seem to run counter to China's historical development. As the Middle Kingdom, China was for centuries the center of civilization, a country where "emissaries of ten thousand states each in his own ceremonial garb vie to pay homage to the crown and tassles (of the Emperor)." Within the country itself, ethnic minorities, however unruly they may seem to the Han majority were quick to adopt the ways of the Hans. Even when China was at her weakest, as when the country was briefly overrun by foreign people during many periods of Chinese history, foreigners readily adapted themselves to Chinese ways and manners. This was not quite true with music. The reason why Chinese music was more prone to the influence of other cultures than was otherwise the case, was that early Chinese philosophers had tended to treat music more as a sociopolitical force cloaked in mysticism in a feudal society than as something which should reflect human feelings and the ways of life of the people. This distortion of the nature of music had inhibited the natural development of Chinese music.

Beginning from the second century the Han rulers after having unified the country in the North, began to push westwards, conquering large stretches of territories contiguous upon Turkestan, and came into contact with peoples of the regions in Central Asia. Foreign music, as distinct from that of the proto-mongol nomads within the country itself, began to flow into China, culminating in the massive influx of the so-called "new sound" during the period of T'ang. In spite of frequent warnings to

nusician playing a Yüan by
ı Ying (1500-1550). Part of a
in is seen lying on the ground.
young attendant is heating
e.

guard against adulteration of Chinese music with this "new sound", the music and dances of foreigners, became so popular that it threatened to replace the indigenous music. We have no exact idea of what this music was like nor how it was reflected in the many large musical forms prevailing at that time. An inkling of it may be had from a sample of "T'ang Music", a drinking song by Li Po "Ch'ing Hai Po" (The Waves of Kokonor), transcribed by Laurence Picken and others from an ancient tablature in the depository of *Togaku* (T'ang Music) preserved in Japan.(15) If anything, the musical example shows how a completely foreign tune could be adapted in the context of traditional Chinese poetry.

The first meeting of East and West (geographically speaking) happily took place in a propitious period when Chinese arts and letters flourished as never before. Rather than treating this foreign music as "cultural invasion", some Chinese rulers looked upon it favourably and indeed encourage it. The slow transformation of foreign musics and their assimilation have taken more than one thousand years, and it was carried on mostly on the level of folk music which has rarely been touched by the formal ritual music of the court. It is important to note that the process of interaction in music has never ceased and indeed has continued with greater intensity as contact between different cultures became more and more frequent.

European music came to China in about the 16th century through the Jesuit priests, and also by way of Japan which was the first Asian country to become "westernized".

China had always regarded herself as the "centre

Landscape with Musician. Jao Tsung-i, contemporary.
e inscription:
e musician is playing a five-string zither,
dding farewell to the soaring wild-ducks.

The inscription: Holding her zither, she is steeped in th
When suddenly appears her beloved fri
Woodblock print.

抱琴方
注想起
到畫眉
郎
紫綬

of the world", but by late nineteenth century she was very much weakened, falling prey to Western powers with the rise of imperialism. During this time the mood of the people was one of fear and rejection, and there was a strong tendency to view Western music as the foreign devils' cultural invasion. Yet this new music from the Western world with its richness in instrumental colours and expressiveness and great variety in form fascinated the Chinese, and was not to be dismissed.

The impact was at first rather superficial, since European church music was not the kind that lent itself to ready acceptance by the Chinese people, and the music brought along by the sailors and merchants was not of a very high order. Still, an inroad was made, particularly in the treaty ports along the coast. Early intermixings of Chinese and Western music produced some amusing results. A revolutionary song in Chinese was set to a tune like "Frère Jacques, dormez-vous", and "O! Susanna" and "Nearer my God to Thee" found themselves in the repertory of wedding and funeral music!

The influence of Western or European music grew as modern schools were established, where group singing and other music lessons were taught. Where a strong cosmopolitan atmosphere prevailed in cities like Shanghai and Tientsin, music conservatories were founded, staffed by European teachers. Besides military bands which were used by the warlords for their own private pleasures and ceremonies, symphonic orchestras playing European classics and ballets appeared in the large cities, mainly for the benefit of the European communities there. In this atmosphere, a "new sound" again intruded China in much the same way as the other kind of "new sound" was introduced into the country in the fourth and fifth centuries by quite another route.

Western music made itself felt in China in more ways than one. Western technology in instrument-making was readily adapted in improving the quality of native instruments, especially in more recent years. This has helped to enlarge the volume of sound, enhancing the tonal quality and prompted the use of equal temperament in fretted instruments. "Silk", once one of the eight kinds of materials for instrument-making (see Section on *Pa Yin*) and synonymous with strings, is now replaced by metal. Purists may frown upon the use of the metal string in place of the silk string on a classical instrument like the *Ch'in*, but actual performance has shown that not only there is no perceptible loss of "flavour" but greater purity of tone and ease of playing are achieved. Chinese instruments made today are quite different from their ancient versions.

In the matter of form, the Chinese musicians are tempted to borrow from Western music what is lacking in Chinese music – large musical forms, harmony and instrumental technique. There is no question that at this stage much of it is still experimental and superficial and that the end result, from a musical point of view, is perhaps not what one would like it to be. Yet, the burden of a civilization of several thousand years must prevent the Chinese from being merely imitative. It is certain that in the course of time, Chinese music will again

抱琴歸去碧山空一路松聲
兩鬢風神識獨遊天地外低
眉寧肯謁王公 唐寅

be enriched by many more kinds of "new sound" and benefited from what is good in other musical cultures without losing its own identity.

◀ Returning Home with My Zither. T'ang Yin, 1470-1574.
The inscription:
Taking my zither, I return to the deserted blue hills;
The wind whistling through the pines fans my face.
Since my spirit wanders outside the universe,
Why should I bow low to greet dukes and princes!

NOTES, REFERENCES and GLOSSARY

NOTES

(1) Li Ch'un-yi, *History of Music in Ancient China* (first draft), Peking, 1958.

(2) *Opus cit.*

(3) Yang Yin-liu, *Outline of the History of Chinese Music* (Shanghai, 1953), para. 167, pp. 73-74.

(4) T'ung Fei, *Fundamentals of Chinese Music* (Shanghai, 1916), p. 88.

(5) Ceremony, music, archery, horsemanship, calligraphy, arithmetic.

(6) *Yüeh Chih* (Book of Music), 1st century B.C.

(7) Hsi Kang, *Ode to Ch'in.*

(8) Transcribed by Hsu Chien, *Collection of Music for the Ch'in,* Institute of Music Research, Peking, 1962.

(9) Transcription from *Illustrations from the History of Chinese Music,* Vol. V, Peking, 1954.

(10) Wang Shih-hsiang, *Notes on the Ancient Ch'in Tune Kuang Ling San,* Collected Papers on Chinese Music, Vol. II, Peking, 1957.

(11) Transcribed by Hsu Chien, *Collection of Music for the Ch'in,* Institute of Music Research, Peking, 1962.

(12) Shen Ts'ao-nung, Ch'a Fu-hsi and Chang Tzu-chien, *Rudiments of Ch'in Playing,* Peking, 1961.

(13) *Illustrations from the History of Chinese Music,* Vol. V, Peking, 1955.

(14) Laurence Picken, *The Origin of the Short Lute,* The Galpin Society Journal, Vol. 8, 1955.

(15) *The Waves of Kokonor,* a flute tablature transcribed by Laurence Picken, Rembrandt Wolpert et al, *Musica Asiatica,* Vol. 1, 1977, Oxford University Press.

REFERENCES

Ch'a Fu-hsi, *Random Notes on the Ch'in* (1954), Collected Papers, All-China Association of Musicians, Peking, 1959.

Introduction to the Collection of Ch'in Tablatures, Society of the Ch'in, Peking, 1963.

Ch'ang Jen-hsia, *The Introduction of the P'i-P'a into China from Western Regions in the Han and T'ang Dynasties,* Collected Papers on Chinese Music Vol. I, Peking, 1956.

Chi Lien-k'ang, *Annotations on the Ch'un Ch'iu of Lü Pu-wei,* Wen Yi Press, Shanghai, 1962.

Annotations on Yüeh Chih. Music Publishing House, Peking, 1958.

Chinese Musical Instruments and Instrumentation, compiled by the Central Conservatory of Music, Peking, 1963.

Collection of Historical Materials on Ancient Chinese Music, Vol. I, *Institute of Music Research,* Peking, 1962.

Collection of Music for the Ch'in, Society of the Ch'in, Peking, 1962.

Illustrations of Ritual Instruments and Ritual Dances of the Imperial Court, 1871, reprinted in 1966.

Illustrations from the History of Chinese Music, Vols. I, II, IV, V, Institute of Music Research, Peking, 1954.

Li Ch'un-yi, *History of Music in Ancient China* (first draft), Institute of Music Research, Peking, 1958.

William P. Malm, *Music Cultures of the Pacific, the Near East, and Asia,* Prentice Hall, 1967.

Robert Mok, *Heterophony in Chinese Folk Music,* Journal of the International Folk Music Council, 1966.

Ancient Musical Instruments Unearthed from the Number One Han Tomb at Ma Wang Tui, Changsha, Asian Music, Vol. X - I, New York, 1978.

Laurence Picken, *The Music of Far Eastern Asia, I, China,* Oxford History of Music, Vol. I, London, 1957.

Curt Sachs, *History of Musical Instruments,* Norton, New York 1940.

Shen Chih-pai, *Chinese Music, Poetry and the Concept of Concord,* Music Research Quarterly, Vol. 3, Peking, 1958.

Shen T'sao-nung, Ch'a Fu-hsi and Chang Tzu-Chien, *Rudiments of Ch'in Playing*, Peking, 1961.

Ts'ao An-ho, *Introduction to the P'i-P'a*, Collected Papers on Chinese Music, Vol. III, Peking, 1958.

T'ung Fei, *Fundamentals of Chinese Music*, Shanghai, 1916, reprinted by the Commercial Press, 1960.

Wang Kuang-chi, *History of Chinese Music*, Shanghai, 1930.

Wang Shih-hsiang, *Notes on the Ancient Ch'in Tune Kuang Ling San*, Collected Papers on Chinese Music, Vol. II, Peking, 1957.

Pan Ku Dance, a Dance Form in the Han Dynasty described in the Ode to Dance of Fu Yi and seen on Bas-reliefs Collected Papers on Chinese Music, Vol. I, Peking, 1956.

Yang Yin-liu, *Transcription of the Kung Ch'e Notation System*, Collected Papers on Chinese Music, Vol. II, Peking, 1956.

Outline of the History of Chinese Music, Wan Yeh Press, Shanghai, 1953.

GLOSSARY

Anyang	安陽
Ch'ang An	長安
Chao Chün	昭君
Chêng (instrument)	箏
Chêng (music)	鄭
Ch'êng Lien	成連
Chêng Shêng	正聲
Chên Yüan	貞元
Chiang Lien	蔣蓮
Ch'iang Ti	羗笛
Chiao Fang	敎坊
Chieh	桀
Chieh Ku	羯鼓
Ch'ien Lo-chih	錢樂之
Ch'ien Lung	乾隆
Chien Ti	簡狄
Chih Yin	知音
Ch'in (instrument)	琴
Chin (a state)	晉
Chin (Duke of)	晉侯
Chin	金
Chin Shih	金石
Ch'ing (dynasty)	清
Ch'ing (instrument)	磬
Ching Fang	京房
Ch'ing Hai Po	清海波
Chiu K'uang	酒狂
Cho Wen-chün	卓文君
Chu	竹
Ch'ü	曲
Chu Tsai-yü	朱載堉
Chui Hu (instrument)	墜胡

Chui Tzu 墜子

Chui Tzu Hsi 墜子戲

Chun 準

Ch'un Ch'iu 春秋

Chung (instrument) 鐘

Chung Tzu-ch'i 鍾子期

Fang Hsiang (instrument) 方响

Feng Huang 鳳凰

Fu Hsi 伏犧

Fu Hsüan 傅玄

Fu Ku 復古

G'ai Sum 解心（粵謳）

Hai Yueh Ch'ing Hui 海月清輝

Han (dynasty) 漢（朝）

Han (race) 漢（族）

Han (state) 韓（國）

Han Hsi-tsai 韓熙載

Han Wu ti 漢武帝

Hao T'ung (instrument) 號筒

Ho 龢

Ho Huai-chih 賀懷智

Honan 河南

Hsi Ch'ü 戲曲

Hsi K'ang 稽康

Hsi Yi Shang 洗衣裳

Hsia (dynasty) 夏

Hsiang 相

Hsiao (instrument) 簫

Hsiao Shih 簫史

Hsien Yü 鮮于

Hsü Chen 許慎

Hsu Chien 許健

Hsüan Kung 旋宮

Hsüan Niao 玄鳥

Hsün 塤

Hsün Tzu 荀子

Hu	胡
Hu Chia (instrument)	胡笳
Hu Chia Shih Pa P'ai	胡笳十八拍
Hu Ch'in (instrument)	胡琴
Hu Yueh	胡樂
Huang Shan	黃山
Huang Ti	黃帝
Hui	徽
Hui Hsien	輝縣
Hui Tsung	徽宗
Jang Wo Wen Ni	讓我問你，讓我聞你
K'an Shu	砍樹，看書
K'ang K'un-lun	康昆崙
Kao Ch'iang	高腔
Ke	革
Ke T'ien Shih	葛天氏
Ku	古
K'u Ch'e	庫車
Ku Hung-chung	顧閎中
Kuan (instrument)	管
Kuang Ling San	廣陵散
Kuan Sê	管色
Kuei Tzu	龜茲
Kuei Fei	貴妃
K'un Ch'ü	崑曲
K'un Lun	昆崙
Kung Ch'e	工尺
K'ung Hou (instrument)	箜篌
K'unmo	崑莫
La Pa (instrument)	喇叭
Lai	籟
Lao Tzu	老子
Li Chi	李頎
Li Chia-ming	李嘉明
Li Kuei-nien	李龜年
Li Ch'un-yi	李純一

Li Po 李白
Li Yüan 梨園
Li Yueh Chih 禮樂志
Ling Lun 伶倫
Liu Yi 六藝
Lo Ku Ching 鑼鼓經
Lü Lü 律呂
Lü-lü Ch'üan Shu 律呂全書
Lung Yü 弄玉
Lungshan 龍山
Mai Chi Shan 麥積山
Mei Hua San Lung 梅花三弄
Ming (dynasty) 明
Mo Tzu 墨子
Mu 木
Nieh Cheng 聶政
Ning (Prince) 寧王
Pa Ch'üeh 八闋
P'ai Hsiao (instrument) 排簫
Pai Hu T'ung Yi 白虎通義
Pan Yen 板眼
P'ao 匏
Pei Wu Yi 倍無射
Pi Li (instrument) 觱篥
P'i-P'a (instrument) 琵琶
P'i-P'a Hsing 琵琶行
Pien Ch'ing (instrument) 編磬
Pien Chung (instrument) 編鐘
P'in 品
Po Chü-yi 白居易
San Hsien (instrument) 三絃
Sang Lin 桑林
Sê (instrument) 瑟
Shang (dynasty) 商
Shansi 山西

Shêng (instrument) 笙

Shih Huang Ti 始皇帝

Shih 石

Shih Ching 詩經

Shih Lin Kuang Chi 事林廣記

Shih Ming 釋名

Shih Yueh 詩樂

Shuo Ch'ang 說唱

Shuo Wen 說文

Sona (instrument) 嗩吶

Su 俗

Su Chih-p'o 蘇祇婆

Su Liu-p'eng 蘇六朋

Su Yueh 俗樂

Sui (dynasty) 隋

Sung (dynasty) 宋（朝）

Sung (a state) 宋（國）

Szu 絲

Szu Hu (instrument) 四胡

Szuma Hsiang-Ju 司馬相如

Ta Ch'ü 大曲

Ta Hsia 大夏

Ta Szu K'ung 大司空

T'ai Ch'ang 太常

T'am S'am 譚三

T'ang (dynasty) 唐

T'an Tz'u 彈詞

Ti (instrument) 笛

Ti Sê 笛色

T'iao 調

T'ienshan 天山

Ts'ai Yüan-ting 蔡元定

Ts'ai Yung 蔡邕

Tso Hsien (King) 左賢王

T'u 土

Tuan Shan-pen 段善本

Tun Huang 敦煌
T'ung Fei 童斐
Tzu Hsia 子夏
Wan Pao-ch'ang 萬寶常
Wang Chi 王吉
Wang Shih-hsiang 王世襄
Wei (Duke of) 魏文侯
Wei (music) 衛
Wei Han-chin 魏漢津
Wen Chi 文姬
Wu 武
Wu Sheng 五聲
Wu Wei 無為
Ya 雅
Ya Chêng (instrument) 軋箏
Ya Yueh 雅樂
Yang 陽
Yang Ch'in (instrument) 揚琴
Yang Yin-liu 楊蔭瀏
Yangtze 揚子江
Yin 陰
Yin K'ang Shih 陰康氏
Yü (instrument) 竽
Yü Po-ya 俞伯牙
Yüan (instrument) 阮
Yüeh 籥
Yüeh Ch'in (instrument) 月琴
Yüeh Fu 樂府
Yün Kang 雲崗
Yün Lo (instrument) 雲鑼

For Transliteration of Chinese Words
the Wade-Giles System is followed.

****